For Leila

Thanks S
fabulous ...

Who Speaks for Earthlings?

[Collected thoughts]

Richard J Deboo

Copyright © Richard J Deboo

Cover photography © Seren Photography

All rights reserved. No part of this publication may be reproduced, stored in a retrieval system, or transmitted in any form or by any means, electronic, mechanical, photocopy, recording or otherwise, without prior written permission of the copyright owner. Nor can it be circulated in any form of binding or cover other than that in which it is published and without similar condition including this condition being imposed on a subsequent purchaser.

ISBN 10: 1497577306

ISBN 13: 978-1497577305

Dedicated to my vegan friends around the world, who inspire me daily and who with each sunrise affirm that around this small Earth there are those with the courage to speak loud for justice, to offer compassion to those who hurt and give love to those who tremble in fear...

We may, today, be few, but we do... speak for Earthlings.

CONTENTS

Foreword: another candle 1

Not like this 5

In a moment there is time 9

My turn to know what 25 years after feels like 12

The ritual of humiliation 16

Distraction 21

The Song of Spring 23

A question of balance 26

Broken words 30

Wait For Me 32

Better than God 36

Circus in the Commons 40

Ubiquity 42

Speech: World Day for Animals In Laboratories, 2009 43

One in a million 48

Poisoned pills 51

The world will eat itself 54

Every little life matters 58

Choosing to die 61

Speech: Animals Count Conference, 2009 65

Extreme 75

The withdrawal method ... 77

Conned-spiracy ... 80

Dark symbols ... 85

Speech: Animals Count Conference, 2010 ... 88

A vegan on tour? ... 96

The withdrawal method II ... 99

I'm not eating THAT! ... 102

Surprised by surprise ... 105

No smart guys in the room ... 107

Missing the (bloody) point ... 113

The gore gore ghouls ... 116

Paedophagia – the sickness of society ... 119

Speech: World Day for Animals in Laboratories, 2010 ... 124

The rise and rise of sanitised violence ... 128

Summer fun ... 132

Speech: World Day For Farmed Animals, London, 2010 ... 134

Yesterday ... 139

Like animals? ... 143

A massacre by any other name ... 146

Who speaks for Earthlings? An evocation of vegan love ... 150

Don't stand by… ... 157

The violence of our vanity ... 160

Between the Devil and the cold North Sea ... 164

A million screams an hour ... 168

Think once, think twice – think life! ... 172

Speech: Animals Count AGM, 2010 176

The sick scent of a lie 180

In living memory 184

The aliens are here! It must be aliens! 186

Speech: World Day for Animals in Laboratories, 2011 190

Metal machine murder 194

The dying and the dead 199

A lifetime lost in a moment's goodbye 204

Speech: Tunbridge Wells VegFest, 2011 208

Call transcript: evidence of truth 219

This Concerns Everyone 224

Speech: Awakening to Animals 2012 (The Politics of Compassion)..226

Animals rights equals human rights equals rights for all animals 244

Three journeys 248

Speech: ARAN, Dublin 2012 251

Remembrance of those who pass before us 255

The mentality that murdered Marius murders millions more 259

Do you know me? 265

Speech: National March for Farmed Animals, 2012 268

Total Animal Liberation – the path of true justice 273

Holding up mirrors in a hall of shadows 277

Equality for all life: a reflection 283

After words 286

FOREWARD: ANOTHER CANDLE

The title of this book is based upon the title of the final chapter of the late Dr Carl Sagan's (1934-1996) wonderful book/television series, "Cosmos", which was called "Who Speaks for Earth?" I have extended that title only slightly to make explicit that my concern in this book is directly with the living inhabitants of this small world. Dr Sagan is one of my favourite authors, and who, as an American astronomer, writer and television presenter, was globally renowned as a great "populariser" of scientific ideas. He thought that it was extremely important to communicate complex scientific ideas to the general public, helping the non-specialist to understand what professional scientists were doing and thinking and to help them to understand the enormous potential of effective scientific investigation. He knew that it was hugely important for the population to be scientifically literate and intellectually curious so that they could better understand, interpret and respond to what they told by the media, by Government and by business interests – including the military.

One of Dr Sagan's most important books was also one of his last, "*The Demon-Haunted World: Science as a Candle in the Dark*" which was a trenchant defence of the scientific method as a bulwark against superstition and beliefs based on nothing more than alleged "insight" and "authority". Like all of Dr Sagan's books it is enormously readable and profoundly important. Dr Sagan is correct when he says that science represents the most successful method humanity has yet devised for understanding the world around us – its results are far more impressive than those of faith-based religious doctrine and other superstitious beliefs.

In that way, he regarded science as being able to hold a candle to the darkness that otherwise surrounds us, shedding much-needed light on the social, political and intellectual landscape. In this respect, learning and education are of great value to society.

We should not allow ourselves to be pacified by those in authority who tell us that "they know best" and we should not be lulled into being mere receptacles for the information that they hand down to us. Everything that we are told should be filtered through the prism of scepticism and rational inquiry. It is vital that we provide ourselves with the opportunity to learn for ourselves, to educate ourselves about as much as we possibly can, and never stop learning, and never stop wanting to know.

Those who are in authority will tell us only what they want us to know to entrench their control and ensure that the system remains fixed to maximise the potential for privilege and profit for themselves... something which is possible only at the expense of the many.

A rational, sceptical response to everything that we are told is the only meaningful response.

I believe that, as well as science being held up as a candle to banish the darkness of religious fiction and other (inevitably profit-driven) "faiths" (such as faith in the financial markets), that we need another candle – the candle of compassion to throw light on the blood of what I call the "meat delusion" – the fantasy that unnecessarily violently slaughters around two trillion land- and sea-based animals every year.

The meat delusion – the lie that says that we *must* eat meat, that we *have* to eat meat, that we *need* to eat meat – is fed to us from the moment we first open our mouths as infants and utter our first cries of hunger and thirst. As soon as they can, parents clog the bodies of their children with the body parts (flesh, lactation fluid, embryos) of brutally-slain non-human animals. They do that because they, in their turn, were told the twisted tale – their minds too were stuffed and lined with the absurdities of the meat delusion.

The meat delusion is hardly ever questioned. It is ubiquitous, its "products" (corpses and body secretions) are displayed everywhere. Our society has so thoroughly engineered itself around the business of "manufacturing" (by mutilating and killing) the "consumer items" (dead body parts) of the meat delusion that it is more difficult to avoid it than to participate in it. No other lie has ever been so successful; no other lie has ever led to the deaths of so many.

We have to take personal responsibility for learning the truth that is hidden in darkness by the meat delusion. By educating ourselves, by choosing to learn about what really happens on our farms and in our slaughterhouses, by wanting to know more about the non-human animals we confine and kill, we can shine a light on the global tragedy of meat and dairy production, something that is also a personal catastrophe for each of those animals who are so cruelly mistreated and destroyed.

We have a choice about what we know and we have a choice about what we do with what we know.

Three years ago (2011) I wrote my first book, "*Nine Steps to Eden: the Humane Route to Paradise*", which distilled my philosophy of compassion towards non-humans. The words collected here are what I wrote next.

The contents of this book are mostly but not exclusively on the issue of the rights of non-humans – there are also pieces on politics, global finance and personal reminiscences. There are short essays, opinion articles, poems, fictions and public speeches that I have shared through my website www.richarddeboo.com and through social media, such as Facebook, YouTube and Twitter over the last few years. The book is designed to be "dipped into" and not necessarily read in a linear manner from cover to cover (although there is no harm in doing so!).

I hope that collecting my thoughts together in this book will help to give voice to those whose cries are rarely acknowledged and whose interests are so roughly dismissed.

There is a cry of agony in many of my words – it is hard to bear witness to intense suffering without being affected, challenged and shocked by what is seen, heard and felt. But there is also hope for I do genuinely believe that we are capable of the noblest of thoughts and deeds and we, as a species, as a society, can change direction, and we can turn from the dark path of violence and destruction towards the open road of kindness and love, a shared journey for all travellers for whom Earth is home.

I hope, therefore, that my words in this and in my earlier book can go some way to lighting the flame of that candle of compassion...

NOT LIKE THIS

It wasn't supposed to be like this, it really wasn't. I couldn't have known that this is how it would turn out, how it would end up.

Ok, so I'm sitting at the back, just staring ahead, looking at those steel bars in front of me, that lock me in here. He shoved me inside, slammed the door on me, locked it, walked away. On my own. Silence. It's cold.

Not how I wanted it to end. Not like this. But what could I do? I'm not to blame for ending up in here, I was led astray. It was others, not me. I'm innocent. I know everyone says that but I am, I really am innocent. I didn't do anything.

I'm easily led, I guess. Too trusting. Too damned trusting. And now I'm locked in here. And I'm not getting out.

I look up to people, I've always been that way. I trust people, I figure they're not going to do anything that'll lead me wrong. They'll look after me, surely? People are good, aren't they?

So I followed. They said, "Come along, this'll be fine." I followed. They put their arms around me, I felt good, wanted. And I liked their warmth, the closeness, the closeness of their warmth, and the smiles. So I followed. I'll do stuff, I'll be good, I'll be right there with you guys. If it's one thing I know, it is loyalty. People are there for me; I'll be there for them. It's simple. I wouldn't just walk off. I don't abandon people, it's not in my nature.

"Come along", they said, "This'll be fine." How could I know that just by going along with them, by going along with whatever they wanted from me, that I could end up locked up, banged up, stuck in here.

Staring at cold steel bars, locked against me. It's cold, and I'm lonely. And I'm afraid.

I don't like feeling fear. I liked being wanted, having people around, having them around, they seemed to care about me; hell, they acted like they cared about me. I thought they gave a damn, I certainly gave a damn about them, I thought we were a gang, together, in it all together, a pack roaming the streets as one, looking out for each other. I was there for them, always there, right at their side. I know what loyalty means, and damn, I thought that they did too. Too trusting. Too trusting. It is cold. And I'm scared. I can actually smell those steel bars, their coldness, and what they mean. I can smell what they mean.

I've not been here long, but I've been here long enough to know. I know what happens to the others, I've seen how they get treated; these guards just don't give a damn, or the other people in charge, their neat, pressed clothes give the lie to their intentions. They must hate us, they really must. It's always horrible but at night, I hear those in the next cell crying out, I hear it in their voice, the fear and the sadness, the sheer, utter loneliness... their voices, their cries are broken, so sad, so very sad... I can smell their sadness, and their fear... they all expect to be next; they've seen others come and go and they think that yes, they'll be the next to go. One day I'll be the next to go.

God, I'm scared.

I didn't think they could do this, that anyone could do this. What century are we in? What kind of a world is this? Ok, we're in here, we're behind bars, but come on, we're locked in, we can't go anywhere, we can't hurt anyone so how can it be right that the "authorities" (although I don't respect their authority, not now, not after all this) can drag us from our cells and deliberately, coldly, kill us? To put me to death? Just dead and done and think nothing of it. How can that be regarded as right? Don't I have the right to live? Don't I have the right to be given my freedom one day? Who the hell are they to decide this for me, and for everyone out there, the lucky ones on the other side of the metal bars, to condemn me, ignore me, let me die?

They asked me to follow, so I followed, but now they won't follow me, and they won't come for me, and they won't comfort me, no-one will comfort me, and if anyone does come for me, then they come for me to kill me.

I don't want to die; heck, I'm only a kid really, just a youth, trusting, innocent, yeah naive, just someone too young, too young to really know, someone who went where others told him to go, and this is where they brought me, into this prison, behind these bars, alone, isolated, cold, terrified.

And I don't want to die.

So that was my life huh? That's gonna be it? That's the lot? So much more living to do, so much more that I want to do, so much else that I want to see and touch and taste and smell, so much joy, love, happiness, so much I can still do, so much I could do ... if only I wasn't locked behind these bars, if only I wasn't trapped in here.

If only I wasn't condemned to die.

Can you call it fate? Was it just an accident, because of where I was born, because of the people around me? Is that all of it, to explain it, how it is that I ended up here? Is it fate or is it hate? They must really hate me, and the others, all the others here too in the other cells, all of us, they must really hate all of us to do this to us, to treat us like this and to just condemn us like that... to let us die, in pain, alone, when there was so much life, so much more living we could do.

But I can't. Damn, I'm cold. I'm scared. I'm sad, so sad, damn I'm so sad.

But I'm a dog, in a "shelter", and they dumped me in here because they didn't want me. Now nobody wants me. I'm a burden and nobody cares. It doesn't feel like shelter, and I don't feel safe. I'm terrified because I know that they'll kill me. Soon they will poison me to death, lethal injection, I've seen it happen, they've done it to loads of us. They lay us down and we die, and I will die and there's no-one to protect me, no-one to save me, no-one to hold me, no-one I can lean my head upon and love them and care for them, trust them and be close to them...

Nothing. No-one. Only this cage, cold, barren, and only my death for me.

Does it have to be like this? Do you suppose it has to be like this?

IN A MOMENT THERE IS TIME

In the time that it just took for me to walk from the kitchen here in my house to sit here at my computer in the lounge hundreds of animals have been slaughtered in this country. Nearly 2,000 farmed animals die every minute in the UK. One billion animals every year, just in the small island nation of the UK.

In the time that it has taken me to write that first sentence thousands of animals were loaded onto trucks, forced and beaten, driven up the ramps, terrified and startled, beginning a journey whose end they cannot possibly imagine.

In the time that it has taken me to pause and look out of the window and watch the trees outside sway gently in the wind, leaves still wet from last night's rain, hundreds of lorries up and down this green and pleasant land continued their trek across the tarmac-grey arteries of the road and motorway system, their "cargo" a frightened population of fearful, tearful individuals packed tightly together, struggling to stand, nuzzling one another for comfort in the noise and terror of their confinement.

In the few moments that it took for my neighbour's car to start and drive off his driveway and take the family on the short trip to the local supermarket, thousands of animals passed between the gates of slaughterhouses, those mammoth, brutalist installations whose only purpose is to take life.

In the seconds in which I watched two starlings fly across the sky, wings pushing against the wind, circling higher and higher and then deftly turning, arcing from right to left, meeting one another in flight, and swooping low to the tree across the road, thousands of new-born chicks, all male, were tossed into refuse sacks, crushed and suffocated to death and thousands of others were drawn alive on conveyor belts to mincing machines, dying before their eyes had barely adjusted to the light of life.

In the moment of time it took for me sit and sigh at the sad loss of their lives many thousands of my fellow animal friends – pigs, chickens, turkeys, cows and sheep – met the machinery of murder in the slaughterhouse, were roughly beaten by the men who man those metal blades and boxes of violence and they were pushed and shackled, punched and kicked and hoisted into position for the final fatal blow of brute force against their gentle minds and bodies.

In the minutes it took for me to eat my breakfast this morning whilst listening to the radio, still tired and only half-aware of the unfolding interview on Radio 4's *Today* programme, death came to those who had so much life and so wanted to live. Killing was the order of the minute, murder was the measure of the moment.

In the seconds that unfolded with the forming of a tear in my eye at the desperate pain endured by those sad, broken souls… "They" carried on killing, and killed again, and again, and again.

In all of the moments that flowed by at the writing of these words I knew that none of the killing had anything to do with me. It was not by me and it was not for me. I did not ask for it and I do not want it. And I will not buy into it and I will not consume the bodies and fluids of the slaughtered.

In a moment there is time for us to revisit the decisions that we make about what we will take from this world. I will not take life.

In a moment there is time for us to revise the lies we are told and turn our minds towards the truth. I do not need to eat the flesh of the dead.

It only takes a fraction of a second to think differently and act differently.

In a minute there is a moment in which we can change the world.

MY TURN TO KNOW WHAT 25 YEARS AFTER FEELS LIKE

It is a fit of memories that shakes my mind to pieces. A brutal rattle of remembrances, those thoughts, sounds and images from a time long gone that bruise my soul and leave me battered, a wreck rolling on the floor, with no escape, no route away from the past, my past that stands over me, overpowers me and shadows my night. But it is I that called my past to me, beckoned it up from memory, for me to wither once more before those days of my history...

Backwards, going backwards, way back to a time when I was younger, so much younger than today, and smaller even, so much smaller even than I am today. There I am, the clarity of the memory a glass-sharp sliver of an image that cuts me, as I am sat on that white chair in the dining room, my father to my left, the dinner plates now empty, and he told me that on this day, this day then, that it was 25 years to the day since his father had died, my grandfather whom I never knew, who was dead long before I was alive. And my father sighed as he recalled the day, 25 years before, when his father died, how he had carried him to his room on that final day, his father a thin, worn man, a brittle sack of cancer, his breathing slow, full of pain, and weary, so weary, life failing within him and leaving him moment by moment. My father was so sad when he recalled that day, now gone by 25 years, when he said goodbye to his father. And I was stunned by the words, stunned by the emotion, and stunned by the very thought of 25 years – I could not imagine what 25 years would feel like, even being alive for 25 years, let alone living for 25 years in the shadow of the death of a father.

Four years on from the time of that conversation at the dinner table, my father died. And now, tonight, as the night hours roll, it will be my turn to know what it feels like to sit there, stare out at the world, and know that 25 years before this day, my father died. My turn to know what 25 years after feels like.

When my father died I did not know how I would, how I could, survive a day, a year, without him, let alone for years and years, and now here I am, 25 years later, and I do not know how I have survived, with those memories, and with that pain that first ruptured my heart and broke my mind 25 years ago to this day.

I live, and I live again with those memories and so I am there, in that hospital room, number 1212, and now how I hate 1212, the rhythm of a number that is a death room, a walled nightmare of suffering and pain. But there I am, in that room, and I am standing, I am sitting, moving around through those minutes and hours. I can hear the unrelenting whine of the fan, the drone of its hum, the turning blades that blew not just air but churned a family's despair around every corner of that space, 1212, 1212, 1212... and I can feel the damp heat that clung to every surface, shocked breathing that spread moisture moment after moment, and my eyes still see the overhead lamp that cast a dulled glow around my father's bed.

And, yes, I still see my father. I still see him as I am sat in the chair by his bedside and I held his hand, and my thumb gently stroked his burning skin. There's only so much that anyone can take, and my father had taken everything that cancer can do to a man, and now he had so little left to give. He had, by now, after a month of blows from the crashing fire of acute myeloid leukaemia and the destructive agony of chemotherapy, fallen back upon his bed, and he could rise no more, the stroke earlier that day that paralysed his left side adding only to his burden that made every breath a mountain of shattering effort.

As I remember, I see as the nurse brings to me that cup of tea, the white plastic warm to the touch, and I hold it with care and draw it towards my father's mouth and with magnificent energy he lifts his head and takes a small sip, a gentle drink to quench the dryness of a mouth that is burned by a suffering no mortal can long endure. My father drank, just a little, but still a little, and lay down his head.

My father was curious, wanted to know the things that were happening around him, as the family buzzed and murmured around him, wandering as we were knowing the inevitable but not wanting to know the inevitable, not believing but knowing, and acting like the inevitable was about to happen even as everyone acted like the inevitable would never happen. This is the paradox of being present at the moment that life goes, gets up and leaves, whatever our fantasy of immortality. My father wanted the family, all of us, to be present; my father the most honest, most practical, most sensible of us all, with all of us dumbed and silenced by this time's truth – we were frequently scattered around the hospital, in waiting rooms, by vending machines grabbing coffees, not in room 1212, not there but elsewhere as though we had all the time in the world, even as my father asked for us all to be there, 1212, 1212, just to be there, because he knew.

How could I not know when I could see, and feel? I sat with him and talked to him, and read out to him from the day's newspaper the latest cricket scores of England's overseas tour – what, surely, could this mean to him, my nonsense, but even then, with a wisdom and a kindness that I can never match, he tolerated my pained youthful struggle to meet the moment, with a gentle turn of his head towards me... and how can I not break again at the memory?

The memories pile up in a car crash of agonies, the hurt of a heart that reaches, desperately, to cross the divide between the one who is dying and the one who, for now, will walk away and go on living. The slow inevitably of the hours that pass and drag wide the divide between the dying and the living. Until there is at last, a last time.

I remember as I stood by the door of the room, that room, 1212, 1212, and my uncle, Mac, now himself long dead, stood at my father's bed and told my father, "Keep it up" (but, after all, what words are there to say?), and now my father was board-flat, prone on his bed, but with immense effort and strength, raised his right hand and arm, his one good hand and arm, and gave the thumbs-up sign to Mac... and how can I not break again at the memory?

Then, of course, I left. I left 1212... I walked towards my father and we held hands and I said, "See you tomorrow" and then I left his bed-side, and walked away from 1212 and left my father on his death bed. How absurd when I said those words, which I knew were a lie, and which my father knew were a lie, but he allowed my indulgence, my lie, he let me walk away from him as I told him a lie, as I walked away and left him to die.

And now, 25 years later, I live with my memory... as it is my turn to know what it means to live 25 years after your father has died. Deliberately, and quite correctly, I have no children to tell my tale as my father told me all those years ago, but in my silence and the seclusion of a personal history, I have my quiet moment of reflection, and I close my hand around itself as – 25 years ago – I closed my fingers around my father's hand... and I remember...

And even now, 25 years later, I break with the memory.

THE RITUAL OF HUMILIATION

I recently had occasion to attend an interview with someone who is disabled through illness for the review of her claim for Incapacity Benefit (IB), a welfare support now renamed ESA (Employment & Support Allowance). Everyone in the UK who currently receives IB has to attend an interview and be evaluated as to whether their welfare support is reasonable or justified.

The process of evaluation has been outsourced by the UK Government to a private, for-profit company, based in France, called ATOS. ATOS are paid many, many millions of pounds by the Government to "process" the claims for these benefits. ATOS are not very good at their job. Some 70% of their decisions are appealed (ie, the claimant is initially rejected for continued welfare support) and very many of those decisions are then reversed on appeal (ie, ATOS got it completely wrong). The great thing for ATOS, though, is that every appeal tribunal hearing is paid for by the taxpayer – their profits remain untouched despite their dreadful decision-making process. So the taxpayer pays twice – once for the initial evaluation, and then again at appeal. ATOS can sit back, smug in the luxury that however bad they are at their job, they do not have to pay for any of the very many mistakes they make.

This particular evaluation took place at a centre in Romford, Essex. The process is designed, it seems to me quite deliberately, to be as humiliating and distressing for the claimants as it can be. This is a process, after all, in which people are judged guilty first and foremost – they are adjudged *not* to be entitled to financial support, and it is for the claimant to prove (to ill-qualified "adjusters" who may know nothing about the condition from which the claimant suffers) that they are disabled or sick and unable to work. Our current crop of politicians despise welfare claimants, believing them all to be malingerers, layabouts, liars and thieves (stealing money from the public purse) and in this they are cheered on by the "red top" newspapers who vomit bile right into the face of any who dare to be ill and unable to work.

At the centre, the interviews take place on the second floor but the building is anything but disabled-friendly (the person I was with needs a wheelchair for mobility). The doors open outwards only, making it difficult to hold the door open and push someone through who is in a wheelchair, and the "press for disabled access" button (to open the door automatically) does not work. The lift is small and cramped, barely allowing room for the person in the wheelchair and their carer.

The "receptionist" speaks in blunt, clipped tones, barely acknowledging your presence, brusquely stating, "Wait over there." The building is air-conditioned but the air-conditioning is not switched on, making everyone feel hot, uncomfortable, drowsy – no doubt to weaken a claimant's "resistance" to the questioning to come. There is a water cooler, over in the far corner, but no plastic cups are provided, making it a sneering mockery in these humid, unpleasant conditions.

The toilet is directly in front of where the chairs face, where everyone is sitting, and staring directly ahead, nervously waiting for their appointments. You have, therefore, to walk to the toilet in full view of everyone and then, when flushing the toilet, the plumbing makes a dreadful, cranking racket, a banging and rumbling of pipes that lasts the whole time after someone opens the toilet door and walks back to their seat. It perversely seems purposely designed to make going to the toilet an embarrassment.

The interview itself has its own purposes, questions carefully crafted to "catch" claimants out about their ability to do work. For example, if the interviewee asks, "Do you watch television?" this seemingly simple ask hides its true intent – if the claimant says "yes" (however qualified that may be), then this is taken as proof that someone can work. The logic is this: if a claimant can sit watching Coronation Street (for example) for 30 minutes, then they can also sit at a computer workstation and work. No mind that it may still be uncomfortable for the person to watch TV, that they may have organised their seating in such a way as to lessen the pain, or that this 30 minute programme may be all that they can manage and one of the few evening pleasures left for someone who is essentially housebound. If you admit to watching any television, then you have committed to being able to work.

Also, "Do you ever have friends come around to visit you?" is not a simple question asking after a claimant's social well-being but is designed to elicit a "yes" which proves (according to ATOS, according to our Government) that if you can engage successfully in social dialogue (in your house) then you can engage in the world of work and participate in the social environment of the workplace. No mind that seeing a friend may be a rare and very welcome break from the mind-numbing, soul-wrenching loneliness of being disabled and physically unable to leave your home, and may be exhausting and leave the claimant in pain after even a short visit from a friend – if you ever talk to anyone else then you can go out and go to work.

And so it goes on. Question after question designed to get a claimant to say "yes" to things that they can do (in whatever limited capacity) rather than being given the chance to say what they cannot do (walk (at all!), use public transport, work continually for eight hours in a day, get to and from their home unaided).

This is a system paid for by the taxpayer to allow a private company to profit from the ritual humiliation of those who are profoundly disabled and even terminally ill (one dying man was told he was able to work just weeks before his death). It allows ATOS to profit from taking away the justified and justifiable social support of those who need it most of all and to dump them at the back of an extremely long queue for jobs, when everyone knows that there aren't enough jobs for everyone who needs one (job seekers outnumber job vacancies by around 5 to 1) and everyone knows as well that an employer will inevitably hire the able-bodied rather than the disabled. But to hell with the disabled, they can just go rot in penury seems to be the message.

The Government claims of course that this process is designed to prevent fraud, but the scale of the fraud is so trivial, so miniscule as to be off the scale – the overwhelming majority of those on IB are rightly claiming that benefit.

The amount of any fraud is pathetically non-existent (less than one percentage point of the total welfare spend) when compared with tax evasion and tax "efficiency" – something that occurs on a much more vast scale at much greater cost to Government finances, with the inevitable adverse effect on public services and national infrastructure.

But would the likes of Sir Philip Green (owner of Top Shop amongst others) who has "made arrangements" to pay zero tax in the UK, ever be challenged by our Government? Would he, and other "captains of industry", leaders in international finance who pay less tax (by percentage of income) than any salaried worker, be ordered to report for questioning? Would they be forced to sit, sweating, in a stuffy, shabby room with not even a glass of water available, and staring at a toilet that makes a bloody racket if they were to dare to use it? No, thought not.

Note: in March 2014 ATOS were removed from all responsibility for the reviews due to their incompetence.

DISTRACTION

One of the common obstacles we face when trying to communicate our concerns about animal exploitation is that we are led (by those with whom we are debating) to talk about anything else *except* the fact of animal exploitation. This is not unique to the topic of animal exploitation but it is a significant impediment to our attempt to discuss the real issues.

For example, when discussing animal farming, rather than the focus being on the farming itself of sentient, pain-sensitive beings, debate is turned towards other matters such as how much room to roam the individual animals have, or the amount of time they can spend outside, or the length of the journey to the slaughterhouse, and their experience when they are taken through the gates of the slaughterhouse. These are important matters (not least to the animals themselves in those situations) but they are ultimately mere sideshows, distractions from what ought to be the only point under consideration: the deliberately abusive exploitation of farmed animals and their premature killing which is, in itself, a moral wrong.

It is a similar case with regards to vivisection, the deliberate infliction of (ultimately) fatal harm upon animals in the pursuit of allegedly viable scientific knowledge. Once again, rather than the focus being on the caging, poisoning, mutilation and killing of these animals, attention is directed towards the size of the cage, the extent of the suffering caused by the poisoning, the interpretation of the results and whether there is a human comparative for the disease/condition under investigation.

Whether the discussion is on farming or vivisection, significant time, attention and energy is spent on debating the methods of the farming and "scientific" research. In those discussions, whose focus is on the details of the practice rather than the legitimacy of the practice itself, this ensures the perpetuation of the belief in the validity of animal farming and vivisection, and in no case would this kind of discussion lead to the conclusion that the practices are illegitimate and should be terminated; after all, what is being discussed is *how* to farm, *how* to poison, not whether one *should* farm or *should* poison at all.

We all know that it is a favourite trick of politicians to answer any question except the one that they are being asked, and those who profit from the animal abuse industry are similarly practised in engaging in debate that essentially fails to debate animal abuse at all but simply focuses on the *methods* to be employed in the continuation of the abuse.

It is incumbent upon us to retain our focus on the *fact* of animal abuse and not to be distracted by matters of *how* to abuse.

THE SONG OF SPRING

The song of Spring
Is a long shriek
A thin scream
That lingers
Through hours of pain

The song of Spring
Is a deep howl
Of despair
A dull moan
A Mother's fear

The song of Spring
With a new birth
A first breath
But right there
The sign of death

The song of Spring
A baby's call
New wide eyes
See Mother
But until when?

The song of Spring
The lamb is taken
Mother screams
And tears flow
Her lamb is gone

The song of Spring
A Mother's shock
Her despair
Unbroken
No comfort there

The song of Spring
The lamb is dragged
Legs kicking
Mouth screaming
A brutal end

The song of Spring
The lamb is chained
A knife clenched
The bloody fist
Punches her head

The song of Spring
The sound of flesh
Ripped by blades
A coughed scream
The throat is cut

The song of Spring
The lamb lies dead
A red mess
Blood and death
Her Mother cries

The song of Spring
In farmer's fields

Mothers stand
Trauma
Can't recover

The song of Spring
A Mother dips
Her heard where
Days before
Her newborn stood

The song of Spring
Delicate sounds
Knives chinking
China plates
And cuts of meat

The song of Spring
The well-fed sat
Dinnertime
Eating lamb
And filling cheeks

The song of Spring
April showers
In the rain
Mothers stand
Drowning in tears

A QUESTION OF BALANCE

Every time those of us concerned with animal protection issues speak out about these matters we are labelled as "extremists" or "fanatics" or even, of course, "terrorists". This is not because of any aggressive language that we use or because of any incitement to cause violence or physical harm. No, we are labelled as "extremists" simply because we demand an end to animal exploitation and killing.

The mere suggestion made by us that we should not eat meat or dairy "products" and that slaughterhouses are places of horror and should be shut down is enough for us to be regarded as extremist. The reason for this is that we are expected to be "balanced" about these issues in a way that no other advocates on issues of justice and exploitation are expected to be balanced. By "balanced" I mean that we, as the advocates for our position, are supposed to give consideration to the opposing point of view and acknowledge that there *is* an opposing point of view and recognise its validity.

On the surface this may seem reasonable. Much of our public discourse and indeed our judicial system itself function according to the principle of adversarial dialogue – person A puts across point of view X and person B puts across point of view Y, and all discussion flows from the exchange of beliefs held by A and B. This presupposes of course that both X and Y are (at least potentially and initially) equally valid beliefs, and thus any audience of listeners needs to hear both X and Y in order to evaluate the (potential) merit of each and reach conclusions and opinions of their own regarding the topic under discussion. Thus, in our discourse we have thesis and antithesis which leads to synthesis (the reasoned compromise between the opposing points of view).

As anyone who watches television and radio news programmes will know, any topic of discussion will likely feature two "talking heads" putting across apparently opposing propositions – although this too often degenerates into a shouting match rather than a considered meeting of minds.

Once again, on the surface this may seem reasonable. But if we dig a little deeper we will know that this is an insufficient mechanism for arriving at the truth on many matters. Not all beliefs are of equal merit or value and in fact the pretence of "balance" and "dialogue" permits dominating beliefs to remain effectively unchallenged.

This is where those of us concerned with animal protection can come unstuck. Any proposition concerning a change to how we (mis)treat other animals in society is immediately countered with the proposition that society *should* continue to (mis)treat animals according to current practice. Thus, when I say that farmed animals should not be slaughtered for their flesh or other body products (and indeed that we should not farm animals *at all*), the counter is that we should continue to do so. My view on this matter is not considered "appropriate"; my position is one that is instantly labelled as an "extremist" or "fanatical" point of view, unworthy of discussion. I am told that I should, instead, acknowledge the validity of animal farming and then discuss *how* to farm animals in ways that (allegedly) best meet the welfare interests of those animals. Then, and only then, can I be permitted to engage in dialogue.

But let us think about this. My position is that I wish to bring an end to the imprisonment, mutilation, torture and killing of sentient, sapient, pain-sensitive individuals. Ordinarily, when discussing matters of exploitation, suffering, violence and killing there is no request to "hear the other side" (one would not even think that there *is* another side!)... but in the case of animal exploitation it is very different.

For example, if someone was to appear on a radio or television programme to discuss the horror of the crime of rape and its effect on its victims, no-one would suggest that a rapist should also appear on the programme to put his point of view across to the audience, and be asked to present his case on the merits of rape, the benefits accruing to him as a rapist and be allowed to question whether those he rapes really are victims – just to provide balance in the discussion. If someone was to discuss the suffering of young children working in mines in, for example, the Democratic Republic of the Congo, no-one would suggest that a mine-owner should also appear to offer his view on the merits of having children working 12-hour days in dangerous, filthy conditions. If someone was to write a blog piece discussing the terror currently felt by the Syrian population living in fear from Government-sponsored snipers on rooftops, I don't think that anyone would complain if the blogger failed to include content advocating for a policy of assassination as a measure for pacifying civilian populations.

But in the case of animal exploitation and killing, the rules are different. It is "extreme", apparently, to want to bring an end to animal exploitation. In a way that no-one who is opposed to sexual exploitation and violence is asked to accept that rape can be a "good thing", and in the way that no-one opposed to child exploitation would be asked to accept child slavery is a "good thing", and in way that no-one in our society would be asked to accept that it is fine for our Government to murder us at will, I (as an advocate for animal rights) *am* expected to accept the ongoing exploitation and killing of non-human animals as very much a "good thing" for society.

Indeed, I am not only expected to accept that exploitation and killing, I am also expected to endorse that exploitation and fatal violence by congratulating farm and slaughterhouse owners for the methods and practices they employ in the confinement and killing of farmed animals. I am expected to be pleased that the confined animals are provided with a little bit of natural bedding and some space to move around a little, and be pleased that their trip to the slaughterhouse is not a *very* long journey and be greatly pleased that when they do go through the gates of the slaughterhouse their killing will be (allegedly) done swiftly and "humanely".

But I refuse to play the game. I will not sanction the exploitation and killing. I would not and will not sanction sexual violence, child cruelty and state murder so why should I endorse the destruction of non-humans? No-one expects me to take a "balanced" view on issues of racism, sexism, homophobia or rape, so why should I be expected to be "balanced" on the issue of speciesism, an issue that is of literally life-ending seriousness for billions of pained individuals?

I do not have a "balanced" view on the issue of animal exploitation – I have the right view. It is a moral wrong and it has no place in a "civilised" society. If I am "extremist" for wanting to reduce the amount of suffering, violence and killing in this world then so be it; I will ever be so labelled. But it is not extreme, it is compassion in action.

BROKEN WORDS

The exploitation and destruction of non-human animals is made all the easier because of the way in which society deliberately corrupts language. Words and phrases are used to disguise the suffering, misery and pain endured by non-humans.

For example, the phrase "free range" when applied to birds such as chickens who are exploited for their eggs and/or flesh, is a classic example of the perversion of language. A friend of mine, AF, recorded some film footage at what is called a "free range" farm, a supplier whose eggs are packaged and sold in major supermarkets. The claim on the packaging of these products suggests that the chickens live happy, healthy lives but the footage shows that this is demonstrably not true.

"Free range" is a deliberately obscure and vague term. It has no formal legal definition and there are no regulatory requirements on the part of the farm owners to treat the animals under their control in any particular way – all that the farm owner has to do is to suggest an "aspiration" towards the provision of (allegedly) high "welfare" standards for those confined animals by providing some access to "outdoors". But whether the animals can "roam" a bit or not (the intention behind "free ranging") they are all confined in the sense that their whole lives will be lived on the farm and they will be killed at the whim of the farm owner. For the vast majority they will still never experience life "outdoors" – they can be locked into vast sheds with thousands of their fellows for the entirety of their lives, with only one or perhaps two very small openings at the ends that a "lucky" few will be able to access. In life and in death, after never breathing outdoor air, they will be labelled "free range".

The packaging on the products and the use of the undefined phrase "free range" corrupts the truth, twists it and turns it upside-down; it despoils language and defaces the reality of what transpires on the farm. And what transpires in every case is the brutal exploitation for economic gain of those who ought to be *free-living* beings. The animals on "free range" farms, no less than the animals imprisoned in the intensive counterparts, are coerced to labour relentlessly to produce "consumer items" (their flesh, milk or eggs) with the inevitable result of this incessant toil being the collapse of their physical and psychological health. This physical destruction – long, long before any of these animals have lived the full extent of their natural lifespan – is the unavoidable and deliberate consequence of this exploitation.

We cannot and we should not comfort ourselves with warped phrasing to belie the truth. I have tired of the mealy-mouthed excuses made by those who stuff their mouths with the body parts of these killed animals and I have tired of the perverse lies vomited from the minds of those who profit from animal abuse. There is no "free-range", there is no "high welfare" standard, there is no "humane" way that freedom and life can be taken from those who should be living free and free to continue to live.

What a corruption it is to lay claim to caring and welfare when misery, suffering and death are the lot of those under the hand of humanity.

WAIT FOR ME

The following poem was written, in a very real sense, by a pig. I saw him as he was being taken by truck to a slaughterhouse. As he looked at me and I saw into his eyes, these are the words that he gave to me.

The ground upon which I walk
hurts my feet
the air that I breathe
hurts my throat
and the things that I see
hurt my eyes
but... do not despair for me
only... wait for me

When the boot is thrust upon me
do not dismiss me
but... reach for me
across the dark of night
and... wait for me

When the fist strikes me
and the punch cracks my back
do not turn away but
look back... and
see me
and see the bruise rise
the tears in my eyes
but do not despair for me
only... wait for me

When I cry for my mother
do not mock me
or laugh at me
but know me
as a youth as a child in distress
who wants only a mother's caress
understand me
and... wait for me

When the bolt to stun me
is held against me
do not forget me
but stand with me
and... comfort me

When the blade is raised against me
do not forsake me
but cry for me
Do not turn from me
but stand for me
beyond the gates that confine me
and... wait for me

Far from the fields I can never know
and below the sun I can never show
my face
for I am locked inside this metal space
where you run your fingers through the grass
just one thing I ask
spare one thought for me
and... wait for me

I will walk where my father…
my mother…
my sister…
my brother…
all walked before me…
where so many walked before me…

through the gates of hell I will be prodded and pushed
and… step by step
I will stand
where so many have stood…

heads bowed…
but I will be proud
even though in fear
when I stand
before my killer

When I am drawn on a chain
to the machine that in a scream
will cut me and rip me
and kill me and spill me
believe in me
and… feel for me

When I close my eyes
with my dying cries
and breathe a sigh one last time
remember this… crime
and
remember me

and even yet...

wait for me

And by the grave that can never be mine

hold a moment for me

in your mind

and even still

I ask if you will

only... wait for me

Wait for me

and one day

you will see me

and hold me

and I will be free

I will stand and I will be free

BETTER THAN GOD

I saw the best (and worst) minds of my generation and the generation past and the generation next wrecked and trashed by a stark, staring hysterical madness of iniquity and stupidity, a cracking up of moral integrity and decency, a decay of mind; all I could hear was the spouting of a ramble, a blabber, a spurting bubble of pus-loaded spittle dribbling from a blooding mouth. A malevolent and malicious cowardice coughed from the throat like a tuberculosis bacterium spinning, twisting in the air infecting everyone in sight and beyond sight with a moral docility, a fragility that fractures the ethical backbone in a thousand places leaving everybody writhing and recoiling on the floor, moaning and groaning – "But I can't, I can't, I can't" is all that they whimper and whine, over and over, and over and over.

Fuck that.

We can do better than that.

Compromise, half-measures and no measures, a meekness and meanness married in a spiteful union of arrogance and corruption.

Fuck that.

We can do better than that.

Backs cowed, eyes lowered, knees bent, heads bowed and the shaking hands reaching in some half-forgotten memory of servility to doff the invisible cap and fingers trembling touching the sweating forelock in shame and deference and to callousness and cruelty.

Fuck that.

We can do better than that.

We can do better than anything, we can do better than anyone. Ever. We can do more, now, than anyone has ever done, ever, over all of those centuries rolled up into the past.

So what of those who went before us, so what, so bloody what? We've not got what we want, we've not got what we should have, we do not have a world that gives to those what they deserve and what should be theirs, their freedom and their life to be lived in fullness, free from the brutalities visited by the powerful upon the weakened.

So what of God or gods as they may be and all the prayers and the clasped hands and closed eyes and murmured words, so damned what of it all, any of it, at all, none of it was good enough at all. We can do better than that, better than God, we can be better than God, do more than God (yes I know: or *gods* as may be... or maybe not) has ever done, did ever do, we can do much more than Him or her or they or it or its, save more lives, save ourselves, save others, love more of the world, save and love the whole world, do more than God, better than God. What Would Jesus Do? Not enough, never enough, never good enough, never did enough, we can be, if we want to be, it's not hard to be, better than Jesus, do more than Jesus.

And Buddha too and all the rest, do better than that, care more, love more, do more and do it now, no self-centred, solipsistic waiting around for eternity, folding ourselves inwards wrapped up, snug in a comfort blanket embossed with words of salvation that can only turn up tomorrow (and we never get to tomorrow) or sit still and dream of nothingness, lazily believing and dreaming that nothing is everything that caring for nothing is everything when that is nothing at all, not enough, only caring for everything and everyone is good enough and don't wait, don't hesitate, don't sit in idle self-reflection or meditation, no contemplation of another place a heaven or a paradise or a nirvana but this place, this one place, the place we can touch and feel and be touched and be felt, the one place that is real, that is really here and here now, and the cries and the screams of agony that batter our eyes and assault our ears are here now, are real now and this place, only this place is the place that merits our action and motivation, the attention of every moment of our lives turned in active confrontation against every corruption and cruelty and wickedness and viciousness that scars and harms and kills the undefended.

So what of those who went before us they are dead beneath us and whether they are shadows over us and around us who knows but no mind and no thought only think now of those who bleed now suffer now need now for someone now to do something for them now to reach for them now and comfort them now and care for them now and love them now and save them now

Do it

Now

We can if we choose if we want to choose to do more today than has ever been done in every yesterday that was and is not now because now is ours now and our words and our deeds and our thoughts and our actions are the only ones that matter now and it is only us now, just us, only we can be the ones who will now after all the failures and the false starts and no starts truly transform and change the world rework the world completely and absolutely

We have to dare to do what must be done is demanded to be done by justice and if we should serve no God or gods (and we should not) nor bow to any man or woman who exalts authority robed in finery then we should know that justice is the measure and justice does not know of any compromise or half-measure only the full-measure only justice fully served is justice at all and it is not for justice to stoop down to our hopelessness and weakness but for us to rise and reach for justice

We can be everything we ever wanted to be and do everything we ever wanted to do and remake the world anew if that is what we want to do and yes it must be done so let it be done let us be the ones who do what has never been done before do not care for before care for now and make the world now into what it should be now

Be more amazing than anyone has ever been before be more in love with love than love has ever been loved before, love more lives and let more lives live than has ever been let done before, say more do more live more love more

And do it

Now

CIRCUS IN THE COMMONS

The UK Government has finally introduced legislation (the *Wild Animals in Circuses Bill*) to ban the use of wild animals (defined as those not ordinarily domesticated in the UK) in circuses after much delay and hesitation, and grumbling about the needs of circus owners and their rights (ignoring completely the rights of the captive animals). The legislation does represent an important step forward but many animals remain confined in misery in circuses around the world, forced to perform "tricks" for the pleasure of the viewing public.

The animals confined include elephants, lions, tigers and camels. All of these species are of course naturally inclined to wander across vast areas in search of food and so their deliberate imprisonment (no other word is adequate to describe their confinement) represents nothing less than physical and psychological torture (no other word is adequate to describe their misery). How can it ever be justified to hold such free-living beings in perpetual servitude for our entertainment? Do those who pay money to attend such circuses really believe that these animals enjoy their confinement and enjoy being forced to perform tricks? And are those who hand over their cash really ignorant of the violence used against these animals in order to "train" them to do as their "masters" wish?

Surely in the second decade of the 21st century we have learned enough to know that this no longer meets the standard of civilised behaviour? But apparently not. Circus owners make substantial profit from having free-living animals in their circuses, and money trumps all other considerations. This demonstrates – once again – that any human interest (however trivial) too often over-rides the interests of non-human animals (however significant).

It is astonishing that some people will still believe that the right of a circus owner to profit financially from the immiseration of free-living animals is far more important than the right of those free-living animals to be free from distress, suffering, misery and pain. This is a despicable and immoral stance but is only one dramatic example of the normalised belief system that the majority in society carry around in their heads – that non-human animals can never have interests that outweigh human interests. Many who are outraged (rightly) at the confinement of lions and tigers in circuses, will nevertheless happily consume the body parts of cruelly-killed animals who also lived lives of immerisation and despair on farms.

It is frustrating that those of us concerned with animal protection have to make the case continually for the equalisation of all animal lives – to educate others that the life of a cow, pig or chicken has equal value to that of the lion, tiger and elephant. All should be born free and allowed to live free…

UBIQUITY

A BBC article from 7 June, 2011 was headlined "The unusual uses for animal body parts", and it starkly demonstrated just how much "use" we make of animal products in our daily lives. We have deliberately engineered a social environment in which animal body parts are consumed in a multiplicity of ways – not just, and most obviously, as food products, but in furnishings, decoration, clothing, utensils and sports equipment.

The BBC article describes this world as "weird and wonderful" but what is masked by this gleeful gawping at the "odd" and unexpected uses to which animal body parts are put, is that all of this is only possible because of the deliberate destruction of a living, pain-sensitive being. What is not evaluated is whether or not the killing of those animals should take place at all – it is assumed, it is taken as accepted, that the killing (most predominantly for food) is okay and perfectly normal... and therefore unworthy of consideration.

Some who read that article may be amazed at just how many household products and other consumer items contain animal body parts as an ingredient, but never question whether any part of an animal's body should be used by us. Still others reading the article, who are perhaps already vegetarian or vegan, may themselves be amazed at just how difficult it is to live a life free from the "consumption" (in whatever form) of animal corpse parts.

What the BBC article shows is that we have normalised the utilisation of the killed bodies of other animals. Some may think that this at least shows that we do use all of the animal and very little goes to waste. But never forget that the animal's life has to be wasted first...

SPEECH: WORLD DAY FOR ANIMALS IN LABORATORIES, 2009

Speech delivered in Whitehall, London, close to the Houses of Parliament, as part of the national march and demonstration against vivisection.

"*I will be as harsh as the truth and as uncompromising as justice. I do not wish to ... speak ... with moderation. I will not equivocate – I will not excuse – I will not retreat a single inch – AND I WILL BE HEARD.*"

Those are the worlds of William Lloyd Garrison, a remarkable man who, two centuries ago, fought tirelessly for truth and justice, to see the abolition of slavery, the vile cruelty that so shamed his era, and he succeeded; and now, two hundred years later we do well to heed his words and fight to end the injustices that are present in our world, to bring an end to the lies that chain animals in laboratories here and elsewhere.

I am standing here today on behalf of the political party Animals Count, based in the UK and now reaching into Europe with candidates standing in the forthcoming European elections. Animals Count is a party that seeks to change politics for the better. And after all that's happened, I'm sure we can agree that politics could do with a change. As a political party, Animals Count is here to represent everyone in the community, including those who are least regarded and most at risk, namely the animals in our midst, whether on the farm, in the home or in the laboratory. And today, of course, our focus is on those in the laboratory.

For despite the promises made by the main political parties over many years, the fact remains that few positive changes have occurred, the number of experiments increases year after year, and we find that protections for animals in laboratories are weakened over time, not strengthened.

A few weeks ago, in the European Parliament, our elected representatives chose to vote through 500 amendments to the Directive that regulates animal experimentation across Europe; and these amendments diminish the safeguards for animals, loosen the regulations and satisfy only the needs of the industry, rather than the animals affected.

Following industry lobbying, our current MEPs chose to accept amendments which include: reducing the scientific justification needed for experimenting on monkeys; allowing almost unlimited re-use of animals in virtually all experiments, including toxicity tests and those causing brain damage, and allowing animals to suffer severe and prolonged pain. How generous of them! Furthermore, the licensing of almost all experiments would be ended – the majority of animal research would become a free-for-all! And all these amendments were voted for by them against the wishes of their electorate, us!

This outright betrayal of the very principle of animal welfare by those presently at the heart of our political system clearly demonstrates just how vital change is. It demonstrates how vigilant we must be, and how determined we must be to ensure that our elected representatives actually represent us. It shows us how critical it is for Animals Count to be there to counter this corruption of power that bows down to every demand of industry, but derisively dismisses the very real needs of the animals that are so used and abused.

This situation has arisen because on all sides we are assailed by a cabal of self-interest – from our politicians, from the captains of industry and commerce, and from the dons of academia, we are beset with only self-serving subterfuge, duplicity and downright falsehood. But as George Orwell said, "In times of universal deceit telling the truth is a revolutionary act." We live in such times and we must be such revolutionaries! Decent, peaceful, law-abiding revolutionaries! And we will do what must be done! At the ballot box, in the boardroom, in the halls of academia and in the corridors of power, we will be there to demand that the truth is told!

We must make sure that the legislators and policy-makers are answerable to us! After all, we have only lent our power to them so that they may act on our behalf. Thus, we must hold them to account and the result of our holding them to account must be that the policy of replacement, reduction and refinement means exactly that. Animals Count wants to ensure that the annual count of the number of animal experiments is a count of zero.

For this to happen Animals Count understands that we need to force the pace of change; it is time to take control of the debate, time to wrest control of the ballot box back from those who would make a mockery of democracy, and time to reshape and remake the world, putting justice, truth and compassion at the heart of our society. It is time to create a world where the pursuit of science and the advancement of knowledge involves no chains and no cages!

Animals Count wants to see now a genuine and realistic increase in Government funding for non-animal alternatives for research, including compulsory training for all researchers in seeking out and using these alternatives. We want to see now a genuine financial contribution from the pharmaceutical industry to implement modern, non-animal research methods; and we want to see now a genuinely independent, transparent public enquiry into all animal experimentation.

Animals Count wants to see now a ban on the genetic manipulation of animals ... and no more cloning! An immediate ban also on the harvesting of animal organs for human use – so-called xenotransplantation. We want to see now the setting of binding targets for reducing animal use in all countries where these experiments are currently taking place and we want to see the establishment of independent sanctuaries, funded by the industry, to which animals can be retired from laboratories to live out the remainder of their natural lives, free from further pain and suffering.

These are the policies that make sense scientifically, and which we know are supported by society as a whole, and these are the policies that should be at the core of the political debate, and should form the heart of the legislation that we make.

We need to see these policies in action now because it is time to look forward into the future, to focus on tomorrow using the knowledge we have today. What we know today is that real progress is made when we choose not to repeat the mistakes of history. And vivisection is a big, bad mistake that should be consigned to history.

We recognise that desperately grasping for and clinging onto the outmoded, outdated claim that animal experiments are either necessary or justified binds us to a discredited past and blinds us to opportunity for the future that can be there if only we do things differently. Can we do things differently? Yes we can and yes we will! Animals Count is here to ensure that another politics is possible because we recognise that Parliament is ours, it belongs to us; democracy is ours, it belongs to us; and the power to make the policy of the government is ours too, the power is in our hands and we will use it!

Animals Count believes in a progressive science and a progressive ethics and a progressive, forward-thinking politics that values the needs and wants of everyone in society with greater, not fewer, protections for those who are most vulnerable and exposed to the dictates and whims of the powerful.

And so, even though I feel sick in the pit of my stomach when I consider those who today are imprisoned and in pain, I also feel that the day of their liberation is closer than ever. Because we're bringing it all together – the research and the knowledge, the evidence and the influence. Our impact on science, law and politics increases all the time giving us the power to lever the scales of justice and tip them inevitably, inexorably in favour of truth and justice, so that in the laboratory the shackles can be loosened, the restraints are discarded and the cage doors opened; so that finally justice indeed is done and their freedom at last is won.

ONE IN A MILLION

One. You are stood at the edge. Paused. Ahead is the field that stretches for two miles. The hot wind beats against your perspiring skin, the sun burns. You are blindfolded. The field before you is a minefield and you know that there is a mine, at least one mine, in every fifteen square feet of earth where you must now tread, where you must now walk without being able to see, without knowing if you are even going in the right direction to make it to the other side. The other side is two miles away ... dead ahead. What do you think of your chances of success?

Two. You wake in a panic, feeling the ice-cold blast of mountain air freezing your skin. You have no idea how you got here but as your eyes adjust, your mind racing, you can see that you are lying precariously on the edge of a rocky ledge, high up a cliff with a straight drop of six hundred feet of space below you. And you are terrified of heights. You cannot look down and you cannot look up; the grip of fear and terror fixes your stare on your hands gripping the cold stone. Above you is sheer rock; below you is sheer rock. But then you do look up slightly and you can see your mobile phone. It's twenty yards away, face-up on the same ledge as your cold, aching body, a narrow ledge, no more than twelve inches wide and covered in ice. Your phone is ringing. That phone is your only chance of survival, your only way to let anyone know where you are, to call for help, so that they can come and rescue you. And to get to it you're going to have to walk along a twelve-inch ice-covered ledge six hundred feet up, hands clasping onto cold, hard rock. And you are terrified of heights. What are your chances of success?

Three. Suddenly jolted into consciousness you hear the ticking first, before you turn your eyes to the right and see the bomb. It's only a small bomb but then this is only a small room in which you find yourself; you try the door but of course it's locked. No key. You look at the bomb and see the timer. Two minutes. A second passes, and then another. The bomb ticks quietly but every tick brings terror to your mind, paralysing your thoughts. Then you see the notepaper in front of you. You pick it up and read – the key to the door is in this room. It is in one of those five hundred small boxes stacked up near the door; each box contains one key. Only one key unlocks the door. It'll take around ten seconds a time to open a box and try a key. The timer says one minute and forty-five seconds. What are your chances of success?

When people think of what needs to be achieved in the animal protection movement to bring an end to animal exploitation, all of that violence and killing, many think that it seems to be like those near-impossible, deliberately-exaggerated hypothetical scenarios outlined here. We know what we want to do, we know what we want to achieve, but it seems a daunting, disorienting challenge with so many obstacles, so much to overcome, so much that needs to be done. What are our chances of success?

We have to be honest about the difficulties that we face but we also have to remember that we have so much on our side, so much that supports the justice and rightness of our intent and much that suggests that though we are fearful, though we are often bewildered by what to do next... we are going the right way, we do have the courage to do what must be done and we will make the right choices.

This is because we know that this is not about ourselves – we are driven by the ethical imperative to do what is right for others, to correct the wrongs we see and the injustices that we witness. The difference we want to make is not for us but for those who – coerced into enslavement – cannot make the changes needed to save themselves.

It does not matter how difficult the task is, it does not matter the severity of the demands impressed upon us, it does not matter how distant final victory may seem to us today… for our determination is unstoppable and unshakeable and success is irresistible.

Therefore do not be daunted by the path we must walk; compassion gives us the courage to reach out for justice and justice shows us that the choice we have made to fight for the liberation of the confined billions is the right choice.

Our task is extraordinarily difficult but so what? In some ways that makes it easier. The great author Sir Terry Pratchett used a neat device in many of his *Discworld* novels whereby if any of his characters found themselves in a really, really tricky situation and the odds were horribly stacked against them, then it was fine if the odds of success were precisely one-in-a-million… if the odds were exactly that bad then they were guaranteed to be successful… I think that Sir Terry was onto something.

Just because it is difficult does not mean it cannot be done; just because it is extremely unlikely does not mean it cannot happen.

And unlike the characters in Terry Pratchett's book we're not on our own with what we want to do… we have truth and justice on our side as well. Daunting and damned difficult it may be, but those fighting for an end to animal exploitation will win…

POISONED PILLS

We have the absurdity of a system that puts pills in the mouths of animals to keep them alive for just a little longer until we are ready to kill them. This is at severe cost to ourselves. Further evidence came to light, in an article in *The Independent* newspaper of 17 June 2001, headlined *"Death wish: Routine use of vital antibiotics on farms threatens human health"*, regarding the nonsensical and dangerous use of antibiotics on farmed animals.

The intensive use of antibiotic medications on our farms has profound implications for human health. This is not a side issue regarding the treatment of animals on our farms that society can safely ignore – the consequences of what we are doing are potentially catastrophic. Antibiotic development (none of it predicated on animal experimentation) in the 20th century represented a magnificent achievement in public health, allowing for the treatment of otherwise fatal infections and making possible even the most invasive surgery, permitting huge improvements in patient outcomes following medical intervention. In earlier centuries it was not the crudity of technique that was the major problem for survival rates after surgery but the impact of bacterial infection after the body had been opened up (or bacterial infection itself in the case of bacteria-borne diseases such as tuberculosis). Antibiotics changed all that, and for the first time in human history provided an opportunity to treat a whole range of infectious diseases and conduct highly-complex surgical procedures.

But with the emergence of what are commonly described as "super strains" of bacteria that are resistant to whole classes of antibiotic medications we would be wise to manage carefully those remaining drugs that are still powerful enough to fight bacterial infection. The acronyms for resistant strains of bacteria are becoming more familiar to the general public – MRSA, VRE, VISA, *E. Coli, C. Diff.* – and the dangers posed to human health are becoming more significant day-by-day.

Without antibiotics we would die from simple infections (as was the case throughout human history prior to their development). Without antibiotics virtually all invasive surgery would be impossible or at least extraordinarily dangerous. Forget organ transplants, forget fixing broken bones, forget tumour removal. Having an appendix or tonsils removed would be likely to kill the patient.

But what are we doing with the antibiotics that we have? We are feeding them to farmed animals who are "raised" in desperately unsanitary, hopelessly overcrowded conditions inevitably resulting in increased stress levels for them with a major adverse impact on their physical health. This results in lots and lots of ill animals whom the farmer is not ready to kill just yet and so they are pumped full of pills to keep them alive for a little while longer. The bacteria in these environments are able to develop resistance to the medications to which they are exposed because of the intensive use of the drugs; this allows each generation of bacteria to mutate and adapt ever better to their ecological conditions, priming them for antibiotic resistance.

Of course it is even more absurd than this. Antibiotics are routinely added to animal feed as a supposed aid to the animals' growth, and so the pills are ingested by healthy animals as well as those with ill-health. And animals are having more antibiotics than humans – in the US around 80% of all antibiotics are given to animals in their feed. This provides the optimum opportunity for the development of antibiotic resistance in bacteria.

Once that antibiotic resistance is present in the population it never goes away. The bacteria do not somehow "forget" how to be resistant; we can never go back to the position where penicillin would be truly effective once more. When the medication becomes inefficient, it stays inefficient. Permanently. If we continue with the overuse of antibiotics on farms the remaining classes of antibiotic will be rendered useless. We will enter a post-antibiotic era in which the most successful medications in history will be confined to history. This will affect everyone on Earth, and it will have happened so that a few people can get rich now (pharmaceutical companies, farmers, supermarkets) and consumers can buy some cheap meat.

What a shocking, ignorant waste. Yet again we see that our treatment of other animals in this world has immense implications for ourselves. If we think and act differently and if we are wise enough to remove the animal products from our diet then we can secure the efficacy of those vitally important medications, retaining them for properly monitored human use only. If there are no livestock then we can keep the pills for ourselves. And then we can live happy, healthy lives.

THE WORLD WILL EAT ITSELF

Readers of "a certain age" may remember a pop band called Pop Will Eat Itself (PWEI). The idea behind the name was that pop music is relentlessly self-referencing, borrowing ideas from its own past and reusing and regurgitating them in new (or not so new!) forms. At the time that PWEI were formed in the mid-1980s the pop music charts were full of cover versions of old songs as well as new songs that "sampled" hooks and lines from other songs – it seemed as if pop music was devouring its own creations and in the process eradicating its energy and creativity, in a terminal spiral of decline. One could easily argue that PWEI had a point and that, whilst some pop stars are still enormously successful today and bask in the adulation of millions, pop music has lost its influence on culture and the social and political landscape. Since its emergence in the early 1950s pop music has never seemed less relevant, less connected with the critical issues of the day than it does today.

And it's not just pop music. One could also convincingly argue that capitalism will eat itself. The economic system at the heart of the Majority World's social systems is locked in an intense battle with itself, which can only result in its own downfall. We saw this during the so-called "credit crunch" of 2007/8, which saw the collapse of some of the world's leading investment banks (such as Lehman Brothers) ... major financial institutions saw the weakness of their competitors and went after them in a predatory attack to wipe them out; speculators and hedge-fund managers betted and gambled on where the financial crisis would strike next and which company would be its next "victim". This predatory behaviour continues today, with traders (working for major global financial institutions) speculating wildly on the ability of sovereign nations to repay their debts (to other global financial institutions), damaging that nation's "credibility" and "credit worthiness" in the eyes of the "market" – the major financial institutions both demanding that debts are repaid (in which case they win financially) and gambling that they cannot do so (in which case they win financially).

Capitalism can only function at all if there is both production and consumption and yet the typical policy demands imposed by the market on what are ostensibly sovereign Governments are to reduce Government-spending, shrink public services, privatise national assets (which are then bought by corporations in other countries), minimise workers' rights and stifle or even outlaw union membership, deregulate financial speculation and decrease public sector employment in favour of private sector employment with fewer protections for workers. All of that is likely only to reduce the ability of citizens in that nation to be able to "consume" the items that are supposed to be produced – and with only limited Government-sponsored stimulus in the economy there is likely also to be less that is produced. Capitalism's policies are deliberately engineered to allow it to reduce competition (the weak are devoured by the strong, as with the credit crunch) which has the effect of reducing innovation and creativity, weakens the ability of citizens to participate economically (around the world many hundreds of millions of people are economically inactive) further restricting a society's ability to meet its own citizen's needs. Capitalism is eating itself.

And now we are devouring the world. The meat, dairy and fisheries industries (collectively we can call them the animal abuse industry) are the most voracious "consumers" of the world's limited resources. At a time when we have the scientific evidence to demonstrate the damage done to the natural environment by the animal abuse industry – the destruction of rainforest, savannah, mangrove swamps, the annihilation of entire marine ecologies, the pollution of groundwater, massive increases in greenhouse gas emissions – our response is to take even more, to want even more meat and dairy to be produced, to burn down more rainforest, channel more water into the mouths of farmed animals, funnel more food into the farm's troughs, trawl ever further, ever deeper into the world's seas and oceans.

We have the absurd situation whereby our obsession with eating more and more fishes has led to "fish farming" – the captive breeding of millions of what should be free-living sea animals in giant containers held just offshore, but with fishing vessels still trawling the seas to catch millions of tons of fishes to bring them back to shore to feed them to the captive fishes.

We are eating ourselves out of house and home. This little world is our only home, literally so. The astronomers have had a look up there and there's nowhere else for us to go… certainly not anywhere that we can reach easily or quickly (quickly meaning within a period of centuries or even millennia). We need, we desperately need, this little world … and yet we are acting as though we can just carry on taking more, and more, and more. This is already unsustainable and yet it seems that our intention is to ignore the enormous amount of scientific evidence that shows so clearly that the animal abuse industry is one of the most significant causes of ecological devastation, and choose instead to stuff our mouths and bellies with more meat, more dairy, dulling our minds to the folly of our ignorance.

If we adopt a plant-based (or vegan) diet, one that is free from all animal-based products, then we can dramatically, radically reduce the pressure on the environment, freeing up huge tracts of land, allowing rainforest and other forested regions to return to their natural state, allowing the seas and oceans to function free from our interference, and safeguard the lives of those other species with whom we share this world. It isn't difficult, it isn't complicated, in fact it's probably one of the most obvious and easy things to do – eat a bit differently and save the world.

It really doesn't matter at all if pop will eat itself, and there's an awful lot of people who could care less if capitalism devours and destroys itself, but it matters, it really matters to all of us, that we look after this world and stop destroying it with every mouthful of flesh with which we grease our windpipes.

EVERY LITTLE LIFE MATTERS

I was sitting outside having a drink at work (we have got an onsite bar on the roof terrace at that particular office, which is kind of nice...) the other day, and a friend of mine, Clare, told me how she'd saved the life of a spider a few days earlier. The spider had fallen into a pool of bleach that she was using, and so Clare quickly took some paper towel and collected the spider on it, and then used more paper towel to gently tease away the bleach from around the spider, until the spider was on as dry a surface as possible. Clare left the spider on the paper towel, wondering if he/she could have possibly survived being essentially drowned in bleach, but when she came back a short while later the spider had gone – it had taken some time but the spider had recovered and gone on his or her merry way!

I thought that that was a really fine, even beautiful story. Not only because of the care and attention devoted to trying to save the spider's life – and succeeding! – but also because of even wanting to save the spider's life. I'm sure we all know so many people who wouldn't and indeed don't give a moment's thought to beings such as spiders, and will happily and casually kill them, just because they are there. Few regard the lives of arachnids as being in any way meaningful or important, or worth spending any time and effort on preserving their lives, but it's fabulous that some of us do, and I wish that more of us would bother. Each spider is an individual being, with an individual personality, and each one is worthy of the life that is theirs.

Clare's story reminded me of the time when I was drinking (yes, drinking again!) outside a hotel in Colchester and a wasp flew into my pint of lager which still had about an inch of liquid in it. The wasp was left motionless, lying on the top of the remaining lager. I knew that I couldn't simply tip the lager out to get to the wasp because that would most likely disturb the fragile bubble of air that surrounded him and was keeping him alive. It was difficult to see how I could easily scoop him out either. I had to gently raise and tilt the glass and drink the remaining lager – watching as the wasp slid backwards (fortunately!) in the glass as I drank what was left. Once the glass was empty I laid it on its side and used a piece of paper that was nearby to roll it into a flat platform so that the wasp could crawl along it and finally get out of the glass. The wasp duly did the necessary and clambered across the paper and staggered (genuinely!) from the glass and spent a few minutes sitting idle on the table, no doubt recovering from the ordeal. After about four or five minutes, he started to flex his wings again and then made a fairly haphazard first attempt to fly and didn't really succeed, but then on the second attempt was back to his normal self and flew off to who knows where. The whole incident was watched by a few others sitting outside having an afternoon drink – none of them said anything, but they must have wondered at all of this fuss over "only" a wasp. So many of us of course will just happily and casually kill any wasp that comes near.

But these little stories should serve to indicate that we can act in a way that preserves life. We can do things, just little things, but things that can help others to live. What we can then do is extend that so that all of our actions are oriented towards caring, looking out for and looking after others, and wanting others to live. Our life can be about life. It does not have to be about death and killing. We can care about the lives of spiders and wasps, and also those cows and pigs and chickens on our farms and those rats and mice in our laboratories. We can care about everyone. And we can want them all to live, and live our lives in such a way that they do not die for us and we do everything we can to let them live.

Saving the life of a spider or a wasp can seem trivial, only a small and insignificant thing. But the power of little things is that each little thing we do does matter and is important... and lots and lots and lots of little things add up to huge things, with the potential to save not just one life but billions of lives...

CHOOSING TO DIE

The BBC showed a documentary in 2011, called "*Choosing To Die*" that involved the author Sir Terry Pratchett, in which he followed two men who had made the personal decision to travel to the Dignitas clinic in Switzerland to end their lives (both were suffering terribly from Motor Neurone Disease). Inevitably, the documentary caused controversy. One of the men, Peter Smedley, was seen taking the final, fatal drink to end his life – a deeply moving and startling piece of television.

The question as to what constitutes a "dignified death" and whether we have the "right to die" as well as the "right to life" (which is enshrined in the United Nations Declaration of Human Rights) raises the temperature in any debate on this issue. The BBC2 news programme, *Newsnight*, had a 30-minute discussion on the *Choosing to Die* programme and argument was certainly lively – at times it was quite cacophonous as the participants started talking over one another, desperate to get their view across without listening to anyone else. Death is an emotive subject...

Sir Terry Pratchett brought a quiet dignity and profound honesty to the programme. Sir Terry is in the early stages of Alzheimer's (a disease which, despite many years of non-human primate experimentation still shows no sign of being cured or even tempered) and has to wrestle with his approach to the inevitably of his psychological decline and whether he will himself make that last journey to the Dignitas clinic. As such, he has brought remarkable courage and also a great clarity of thought and emotional integrity to these discussions. But whether or not he will make that personal decision himself to travel to Dignitas, Sir Terry clearly believes that the UK should offer the same opportunity to

British citizens here in the UK as is available in Switzerland (after all, it is a considerable expense – around £10,000 – to travel to Dignitas to die). Many others agree and they too want to see the UK offer the "right to die" for those who are of "sound mind" and who suffer from a terminal or incurable disease. Who, after all, is the "owner" of a life if not the possessor of that life? Many regard a slow, painful decline and death in hospital or a hospice with horror and would prefer their death to take place at a time of their own choosing, in a place of their own choosing.

The key concept of course is choice – the idea that we should be able to choose for ourselves the moment of our exit from life. And this is where the controversy arises. We talk often about the "right to life" (enshrined in international law) and indeed the "sanctity of life" is the more usual phrase spoken, which brings to mind the cultural effects of religious traditions and the idea of the "divine" element of the life-force. Life, we are told, has intrinsic value – it is not instrumental (ie, my life has value *because* I do X) and it is not conditional (ie, my life has value only *if* I do X), it has value simply because it is. The fact of possessing life is enough to grant value to that life. Many in society believe, therefore, that to want to deliberately end that life is to "violate" our "covenant" with life itself. To make life-ending actions lawful would, many feel, irreparably corrupt our society and establish a precedent that places many more people at risk of fatal harm. Life, we are told, is valuable, so valuable in fact that there is no "choosing to die"…

So it is that in the UK at least our acts and our laws demonstrate our desperation that everyone should live for live for as long as possible (even if in terrible pain, distress and discomfort). We devote enormous time, money and energy in keeping alive people who are suffering from incurable or terminal diseases, desperate as we are to keep someone alive (even if against their own wishes) for one more day, and then one more day if we can, and then one more day if possible, even if they are pumped so full of drugs that not only is their pain soothed a little but also renders them insensible, essentially unaware of anything or anyone around them. This is the "right to live" in all its glory.

But I like to look at this issue in its widest context, and see how dramatically this contrasts with the lives and deaths of non-humans in our society. It is immediately apparent that the "right to live" is reserved only for human members of the world community. Non-humans, whether animals confined on farms or laboratories or animal companions in the home or living in the "wild", do not have a right to life and any "choosing to die" is a choice made by us on their behalf. An animal companion in the home can be killed simply because his or her "owner" has tired of them and wants them to die. I know veterinary surgeons who have had to kill an animal under precisely these circumstances – a healthy being put to death at the whim of another...

And, of course, those animals on our farms and in our laboratories exist in an environment that will be deliberately fatal for them. We choose not only how they live (often in appalling conditions) but also how and when they die as well (very often in conditions of extreme terror and violence). They have no right to life, and their lives have value only in so far as they are of economic (or other) value to us; the animal's life has no intrinsic value – it is instrumental (they can live only because we can use them) and it is conditional (they can live only if we can get something from them). It is the polar opposite of how we regard human lives. A non-human animal can be done to death whenever we choose, for whatever reason we choose, and however we choose. It does not matter if the death is painful (psychologically and physically) and it does not matter if the animal is healthy and it does not matter if the animal could live for many years to come – nothing matters except the brute fact that we want them dead.

This is an absurdity – at the same time as denying that humans can choose for themselves that they can die because of their extreme pain and suffering, we deny life to those animals who are in no pain, not suffering and have so much life in them.

The law should change to grant to humans the right to die at a time and in a place of their own choosing and at the same time grant to non-humans the right to live.

SPEECH: ANIMALS COUNT CONFERENCE, 2009

Today... we are... what the future will be like. The choices we have made already, about the food that we eat, our consideration for the environment and our empathy towards other animals with whom we share this world, these are choices that will also be made by the overwhelming majority in our society, and a compassionate and environmentally-sensitive lifestyle will be regarded as... simply ordinary, just what people do.

There will be a time when those who will come after us will look back upon us to our time and they will despair at the damage and destruction we wrought upon the rainforests and savannahs, for the sake of one more beef-burger. They will despair at our determination to dredge the seas and oceans and drag up from the deep all forms of life for the sake of one more bag of cod and chips, a tuna sandwich or a bowl of shark-fin soup. They will look back in horror at the killing centres we call factory farms and slaughterhouses, the vast mechanisation of violence, the industrialisation of brutality and cruelty, constructed and managed at immense expense simply for the sake of a "turkey twizzler", "chicken pieces" or a dozen eggs or a pint of milk.

They will look back and be outraged, shake their heads in disbelief that it was ever like that and be grateful and relieved indeed that they live in their time, when it is most assuredly not like that anymore.

We... alas... are not there. We are here, in our time, when it is still very much "like that". But for the sake of ourselves, for those other species whom we cause so much harm and for protection of the planet... change must come, and we must force the pace of change. We must bring the future into the present.

And Animals Count believes that change – meaningful, effective change – will take place through engagement with the legislative and political process.

This is because we recognise that all of the things we currently do to other species – livestock farming, habitat destruction, vivisection, blood sports, and so on and so forth – are all done because the legislation, the laws of our society and the political structures and social policies that guide and decide those laws, all say that it is all ok.

All of those things can be done because it is legal and socially acceptable to do so. Because it has been agreed that those others, those mere non-humans, are so much lesser than us, they are regarded as commodities, as property, as objects only, to be used as we choose and their lives lived absolutely according to our wants, our needs and not theirs, and their deaths decided when and how it suits our purposes, when the greatest economic advantage can be achieved through their physical destruction. It has been agreed that they are simply life unworthy of life.

I disagree.

I accept none of those things.

I believe and think differently, and I believe and think differently because I have listened to and learned from all of the evidence around me, that tells me so clearly that each of those others is the owner of their own life, a life that can be lived utterly independently of what we may want; each has a profound, rich and complex inner world that knows pain and suffering, but also pleasure and happiness, and every one of those others wants only to be free to live his or her life according to his or her needs. I know that they are truly life worthy of life.

And I also know that there are many, many, many people who do not think like that. I know that the way that I think and the way that all of us here today think, is a rare, an uncommon, way to think. But that is of no great consequence.

Because it was the case at one time that it was regarded as odd in the extreme to believe that there should be no slavery in our world, that it should be impossible for the complete life of a person to be wholly-owned by another. But slavery was endemic in societies across the world for millennia, with illustrious and enthusiastic supporters such as Plato and Aristotle, whose works – adorning the Classics section of any library or bookstore today – give fulsome praise to the benefits of slavery and slave-ownership. Those who, at the time of Plato and for many centuries after, fought against the practice of slavery were derided, ridiculed and dismissed as fantasists.

And yet today we regard with abhorrence the very notion of slavery.

It was the case at one time that it was regarded as odd in the extreme to believe that women, the "fairer sex", could possibly have capacities that matched those of men, or could possibly be entrusted with decision-making powers. Indeed, classic Christian theology denied that females could have a soul – they were simply not equal to a male, and were certainly lesser, they said, in the sight of God. Those who, over the centuries, fought against this gender prejudice and dared to suggest that women were equal to men were derided, ridiculed and dismissed as fantasists.

And yet today we regard with intense displeasure the very notion of gender discrimination.

It was the case at one time, and not too long ago, in what they called "the land of the free" in the United States, a country founded upon the principle that "all were created equal", that some were, in fact, more equal than others, and when it came to skin colour, black most definitely did not equal white. It was normal, they said, to segregate a society on racial grounds, imposing poverty and deprivation upon a large proportion of the population purely because of their skin pigmentation. Those who, for so many years, fought against this racial prejudice and dared to suggest that black was of course equal to white, were derided, ridiculed and dismissed as fantasists.

And yet today we regard with justified anger the very notion of a racial discrimination.

And so... we can see... that beliefs that at one time were seen as abnormal, absurd and against all the norms and values of society, became, in fact, the norms and values of society and such beliefs are seen today as normal, sensible and absolutely consistent with being civilised, rational and compassionate.

Today we criminalise the act of enslavement of one person by another, we criminalise the acts of racial and gender discrimination; where once our society condoned the oppression of the weak by the strong, this is now condemned, and our laws are set to ensure that such oppression can never again be used by the powerful against the defenceless.

Therefore, when we see that today society condones the profound oppression, exploitation and destruction of animals in farms and laboratories and regards those animals as nothing more than economic units, as objects that are just consumer products, we do not need to despair and nor should we, though we may allow ourselves a moment of sorrow to reflect upon the extreme suffering and pain endured by so many.

We must understand that change will come and society will condemn the viciousness of our factory farms and slaughterhouses, the absurdity of serried rows of animal body parts displayed in packets and cartons on supermarket shelves, the horror of the deliberate infliction of physical mutilation and fatal illness on healthy animals in laboratories allegedly in the pursuit of science, the wanton cruelty of blood sports in the pursuit of entertainment. All of that will one day be condemned as an outrage, as an aberration, the expression of an uncivilised, backward society that should have known better and chose not to know better.

Our world will emerge from the shadow of this moral darkness and we can, indeed we must, be those who will guide society towards a future where compassion for all those with whom we share this world – humans and non-humans alike – is regarded as the starting point, the foundation and the benchmark of civilisation.

And how this is achieved is surprisingly simple.

The evidence is there, the research has been done, the knowledge has been gained to tell us all about the rich, complex lives of other species, the colossal failure over decades of all forms of animal experimentation, the profoundly negative impact on the environment of meat and dairy foods for human consumption, and the gravely harmful effects of those meat and dairy foods on human health.

The four conclusions to be drawn from evaluating the evidence are inescapable:

- "farming" sentient, pain-sensitive beings is morally unjustifiable and furthermore is wasteful of the very limited land and water resources available

- experimenting on sentient, pain-sensitive beings is morally unjustifiable and furthermore fails the basic principles of science and holds back medical progress

- eating meat and dairy foods is incompatible with slowing down or reversing climate change and global warming – irrespective of any other measures that are undertaken

- eating meat and dairy foods damages human health; such an unnatural diet destroys human vitality and has a huge economic impact on healthcare systems and workforce productivity

We know these things to be true. These truths are consistent with all of the evidence.

What we must do now is to marshal the evidence and engage with those who have the power to legislate to force through change, and to become those who have the power to legislate and make change happen, change that is essential for human health, animal health and the health of our planet.

We must understand that to create change we must have clear objectives in mind, not just raising awareness of these issues, but to have practical solutions to offer as an alternative, not just to say what we do not like about the current situation, and we must be able to express precise, workable and defined policy proposals to replace the present framework.

It is not enough simply to add our name to yet another online petition, to join yet another *Facebook* group, to *Twitter* against the perceived evils of the animal abuse industry and to believe that by so doing all will be made well in the world.

We know what we want, we know what needs to be done, we know what the future should and indeed will be like; the demand now is to find realistic and achievable methods to bring that future closer to us.

Animals Count can create a way to do so, can force a path through the present to pave the road that we can all walk to arrive at that better future. Animals Count are not here simply to make up the numbers, to be just another voice for the animals. Animals Count are here to make history happen.

What we understand when we look back to radical change that has taken place in society, from the abolition of slavery, the emancipation of women, through improvements in child welfare and protection, to the end of discrimination on grounds of gender or race, all such changes have come about through political pressure being brought to bear upon those in charge, pressure which exploded through the corridors and chambers of power, leaving a very different world in its wake.

To achieve what we want, we have to recognise and use the power that we have, for the future is ours and belongs to us and it is with our hands that we will shape the future and build that better world.

For whilst, on the surface, our political leaders may seem to regard us with disdain and disinterest, in truth they are nervous, they are wary, indeed they fear us. They know the truth that the power that they have has only been lent to them by us; it is ours to give and it is ours to take away.

We simply have to understand that and organise and mobilise ourselves to challenge and defeat their failed and destructive policies – we must be there at the ballot box and in those halls of power to demand that our demand for real and lasting change is heard.

We have an extraordinary opportunity to be the standard bearers for a better future. We are those who are best placed to inform, to educate, to offer a practical alternative to the current system which is in disarray.

For example. We recognise that massive reform, indeed a wholesale re-engineering, of the agricultural system is long overdue and if we do that it can bring enormous economic benefit to our society. We understand that the wasteful livestock farming and fisheries trades are utterly unsustainable and only survive with huge financial subsidy from the public purse, which hides the real costs of those damaging industries. Supporting those trades is no longer supportable.

Why would we want to continue to support failing industries, that are causing the collapse of ecologies on land and sea, here and around the world, at vast financial, community and environmental cost, when it is, in fact, so simple to promote and provide for alternative practices?

Removing all such unnecessary subsidy and providing investment instead to sustainable crop agriculture will allow for far more effective management of our limited land and water resources. This will free up very substantial financial capital which can be refocused and retargeted towards other pressing social concerns such as education, healthcare and welfare, and urgent environmental concerns such as the recovery of failing land and sea ecologies, protecting biodiversity and safeguarding natural habitats and wildlife.

No-one needs to lose out, and in fact, everyone will win. Through the availability of finance that no longer need be poured into the seemingly bottomless hole of subsidy for unsustainable livestock and fisheries farming, investment becomes possible for more productive agriculture and industry, substantive support for entrepreneurship and developing new business, and education and training for those moving into these new employment opportunities.

That is what progressive politics is all about. That is what forward-thinking, long-term social policy is all about. That is what a better future for everyone is all about. That, in fact, is what Animals Count are all about.

It no longer has to be about just Conservative, or Labour, or Lib Dem. It does not have to be about the negative, vindictive, dead-end politics of UKIP or the BNP. **Another politics is possible**. Animals Count are here to be the difference that makes the future possible, that makes the future happen.

The Animals Count manifesto is the most radical, most complete, most workable manifesto ever put together in the field of animal protection politics. Alone of all the political parties, Animals Count have the courage, the backbone and the determination to say what must be done and how to do it and will be there to see that it is done.

We can break the mould. The current system is in drastic decline, its philosophy is discredited and its proponents are bankrupt of ideas and hope; they offer only more of the same that has failed us all for decades.

Animals Count are here to break through this corrupted and damaged system, contaminated with scandal, dishonour and outright thievery, and we will go beyond the broken-down, run-down, squalid and inadequate policies of our so-called main political parties, whose members are interested only in power for its own sake and securing for themselves privilege, patronage and self-satisfied luxury at the expense of the many, whilst occasionally tossing down a scrap of a policy or two to the masses to keep them passive and quiet. Animals Count will not be quiet. We will not be passive. **We know that another politics is possible.**

This world deserves better, those other species deserve better, and we deserve better. Let us therefore work together to make this world a place of sanctuary and security for everyone in our society, where the needs and wants of all are valued and upheld, and our civilisation is at last based upon the civilising principle of compassion.

There must be political elections in the United Kingdom in 2010. And Animals Count must be there to contest those elections. With your support we can begin to bring the future into the present. So can we be the ones to make change happen? Yes we can and yes we will!

Thank you.

EXTREME

Am I an extremist? The claim is set against me. Recently I have received vitriolic and insulting messages because of my belief system set out on my website (www.richarddeboo.com) and in my book, *Nine Steps To Eden*. My belief system is very clear – I want an end to non-human animal exploitation (it goes without saying that I want an end to human exploitation too). I want to see no more animal farming, no more vivisection, no more hunting, no fishing, no more fur farms. No meat. No dairy. No livestock. An end, a final end, to all exploitation of all other animals with whom I share this small world.

For this I am labelled as an extremist. But why? If we stop, and pause, and think about what I am asking for, then it really should not be seen as "extreme". The world that I want to see would have less suffering, less pain, less bloodshed, less violence, less cruelty, and less killing. The world that I want to see would offer better protection for what remains of the natural environment and would lead to a recovery in the biodiversity of the land and marine ecosystems. The world that I want to see would lead to improvements in human health, as people would be eating more naturally healthy foods, reducing the likelihood of often fatal illnesses such as heart disease, diabetes and many cancers.

So the world that I want to see would offer something better for non-human animals, for the planet and for ourselves. It is win-win-win all the way. The world that I want to see is about caring, about compassion, and about life.

Is that extreme?

We have, of course, simply normalised the exploitation and infliction of massive physical and psychological trauma on and violent killing of animals. Destroying animals is what we do (well, most of us don't and wouldn't but are happy that others do it for us, on our behalf), and it's what we want to do. The "naturalness" of destroying animal lives is never questioned, and so when I do question it, with my book and my website, this causes quite a reaction in some people, responding to me in a verbally aggressive and hate-filled manner.

Yes I am questioning their belief in what I describe as the "meat delusion" but that is all that I am doing. I have to wonder just what it is that they are afraid of that they should react so badly. Maybe, subconsciously, they are afraid that I am right. By simply being alive I (and my many millions of fellow vegans) have already proven that one can live quite well and indeed be fully healthful and positively thrive on a diet that contains no animal products. The evidence of science demonstrates the profound agony suffered by other animals at our hand. It is, I feel, impossible to justify morally the intense pain endured by those billions.

So yes, maybe, just maybe, I am right to call for the end of animal exploitation. Is that such as a bad thing? Is it so awful to bring an end to the deliberate killing of billions, and to stop the premature deaths (by entirely preventable illnesses) of millions of people, and to want to protect what remains of our rainforests, savannahs and marine environments?

Is it really so "extreme" to want everyone to live and to live well?

THE WITHDRAWAL METHOD

One of the common reasons people give for not adopting a vegan diet is that one is too used to eating meat and dairy products. People say that they don't know what to eat or drink instead. They say that eating animal-based foods is just what they do and they wouldn't know how to go about doing things differently.

They believe that it's too difficult to "go vegan". But really, it's not that difficult at all. Certainly it's now much easier than in the past with the wide availability of vegan items on the Internet, more health food stores than ever before, and supermarkets now labelling their "vegan-friendly" products.

So what is really stopping people is not access to vegan foods and other consumer items, it is behaviour. We are brought up to eat meat and dairy and this is reinforced throughout our formative years and becomes normalised in our day-to-day activities. When we grow up and become consumers ourselves this reinforced behaviour is repeated over and over when we shop for food and other products. Buying animal-based foods is embedded activity and most people not only don't think about alternatives but wouldn't choose them even if they did. They won't choose them because they don't normally choose them. Behaviour is fixed and, in a way, people are "addicted" to that behaviour because they have conditioned themselves to so behave.

How then to get people to "withdraw" from the behaviours that normalise the consumption of meat and dairy? How do we get people to change? In fact, it is not nearly as challenging as it may appear.

We act as though it is difficult to change, to behave differently, only because we have convinced ourselves that it is difficult to change, when really it is not difficult at all. It is simply a matter of modifying what we do, by thinking ahead about what we will do differently tomorrow compared to what we have done today. By simply planning change we can make change happen.

Here is a personal example. For way too many years I drank way too much coffee at work. Every day, I would drink an average of a dozen or so cups of black coffee, in just eight hours. I knew for a long time that that really wasn't doing me any favours at all, and then at the end of 2010 I figured that seeing as how I knew that, then I ought to do something about it! So, I thought differently and decided that the next day, at work, rather than getting a coffee as soon as I walked in the building I would get a cup of water instead, and I would have a bottle of water with me (filled from the tap) so that I always had something to drink, something that wasn't coffee. So that's what I did: the next day at work, I drank zero cups of coffee instead of twelve. And then just incorporated that behaviour into my routine. No coffee, just water instead. And I've carried on doing that ever since, and now I never think about getting a coffee – I just get water; that's what I do and it's completely "normalised" behaviour, just like getting coffee used to be. Change is both possible and simple.

We can all do the same, with everything that we eat and drink, and buy, reconsidering the things that we will spend our money on. Just because we are used to buying meat or milk at the supermarket (just as I was used to drinking coffee as soon as I walked in the door at work) doesn't mean we have to do the same thing the next time. We can plan to do our next shopping trip a little bit differently, avoiding the meat aisle (as I avoided the coffee machine!) and wander across to the "free from" or "veggie" section instead, and rather than buying cow's milk we can buy soya or almond or rice milk: it still does the same thing, fulfils the same function, it's just a little bit different.

By withdrawing from our conditioned behaviours we can make a major difference, not only to ourselves but to others as well. I feel better for not drinking over a dozen coffees a day, and I think that people would all feel better if they didn't eat meat and dairy foods. And in that case it wouldn't only do us some good but would of course be so much better for the non-human animals as well...

CONNED-SPIRACY

Conspiracies are everywhere. The Internet is awash with conspiracies. No-one believes anyone. Everyone thinks that everyone else is lying. Distrust and mistrust stalk society. Governments and big business and the military are all in it together, telling us nothing but lies.

9/11 must have been an inside job. 7/7 must have been an inside job. The war in Iraq was a conspiracy. The war in Afghanistan was a conspiracy. People still talk about JFK 50 years after the event.

Marilyn Monroe was murdered by the mafia... or by JFK... or by RK. Or was it Mossad or the CIA who pulled the strings of RK or JFK or maybe both? Alien UFOs are hidden in Area 51. "Man" never landed on the moon, but aliens landed in ancient Egypt and built the pyramids. And they're still here: the British Queen is an alien reptile and eats human babies. President Obama is a human but he is not an American.

Elvis faked his death. So did Jim Morrison. Kurt Cobain didn't fake his death but *he* didn't pull the trigger.

Television is a mass hallucinogenic to dupe the masses into a stupor of apathetic submission. That one must be true because I saw a programme on the telly about it.

Radio waves cause cancer. Mobile phones cause cancer. Plastic causes cancer.

Cold fusion is real, but global warming is not. Any floods are caused by God, even if God is dead because religion is just an opiate of the masses.

The Bullingdon Club is the Bildberberg Group who are the *Illuminati*, just as described by Leonardo da Vinci. And behind the scenes pulling strings are the descendants of Jesus, even if Jesus was gay, or a mushroom, it's hard to say. All we can say is nothing is as it seems.

Conspiracies are "here, there and everywhere" – which is a song title by Paul McCartney who, *in fact*, died at the age of 27 in 1969; remember, he would have been "28 IF" he had lived, according to the number plate of the Beetle car on the cover of the Abbey Road album. The late Paul McCartney was replaced by a look-a-like, sound-a-like, write-a-like (but forget "*Silly Love Songs*")...

People will believe anything – except "official versions". Official versions are all lies.

Except...

People will not accept the biggest conspiracy of them all – the meat delusion. People are told by Governments and big business that they absolutely should consume meat and dairy, and lots of it, and more of it, and even more of it, and if you fall ill you should just pop pills and have surgery, those pills and surgeries that have been tested (but certainly not perfected) on non-human animals. People are told by multinational pharmaceutical companies ("Big Pharma") that those animal experiments are necessary and that the pills and the surgery are the way to go to beat heart disease and cancer and diabetes and all the rest.

And people believe all of it.

All of a sudden everyone wants to believe in what Government and big business and Big Pharma are telling them. It can't possibly be the case that *their* self-interest would lead them to tell lies about whether we need to eat any meat or dairy. It can't possibly be true that animal experiments are a waste of time and lives (human and non-human). It can't possibly be true that heart disease and many cancers and diabetes can be prevented and even reversed (if it's already occurred) and eradicated by diet, by simply switching to a plant-based diet. It can't possibly be true that meat and dairy are harmful to our health. It can't possibly be true that human beings can live healthy lives without ever eating any meat and dairy, ever. It can't possibly be true that the fishing industry is the worst of all industries for the health of our seas. It can't possibly be true that we waste billions and billions of pounds annually subsidising and supporting meat, dairy and fisheries industries which would otherwise go bankrupt because they are so catastrophically unsustainable and wasteful. It can't possibly be true that the animal abuse industries represent *the* major cause of global ecological damage and climate change. It can't possibly be true that all the animals on all the farms and in all the slaughterhouses and all the laboratories are mistreated and abused. It can't possibly be true that humane slaughter does not exist.

No, none of that can possibly be true because the Government and big business and Big Pharma, meat producers and dairy farmers and the medical industry are all telling us it's not true. And they would never lie. They would never tell us something that's not true just because they can make billions and billions of pounds in profits if we continue to buy into what they tell us, if we buy just what they tell us to buy.

The meat, dairy and fisheries industries and the associated exploitation of non-humans in "biomedical research" represent the most successful conspiracy in human history – almost the entire society in which they function has bought into the deliberate corruption of the truth, the wilful misrepresentation of the scientific evidence and the consequent successful promotion and production of "consumer items" purchased in massive quantities, because that's what people are told to consume by those who profit most if we do indeed continue to consume all that they produce.

We are talking about 60 billion animals dead. Every year. Two *trillion* dead every year when we include all of the sea-lives killed. All of those individuals contained in that vast number each suffered a desperate, painful and violent death. And none of them – none of them – **had** to die. Slaughter for profit on an unimagined scale.

But when I tell that to people, many of them respond with a shrug of the shoulder or an uncomprehending, blank stare. They do not want to believe that they do not need to eat meat, and they do not need to eat and drink dairy, or swallow "oily" fishes, and they do not have to pop pills to have a healthy heart. They refuse to refuse the products of the animal abuse industry. They do not want to see the devastated rainforests and near-empty seas, caused by the animal farming industries. They do not want to hear the scream of pain from the farm and the slaughterhouse. They do not want to call a corpse a corpse.

I can only imagine that so many do not want to see and hear and know because they have been taught to believe in the meat delusion, and because they cannot believe that anyone would ever lie to them about something so serious as the destruction of their own health and the health of the planet and the violent killing of billions. And, perhaps, it is because they cannot comprehend or want to believe that they participate in, and are responsible for, such immense pain and devastation caused to so many. But people have been conned. And it's the most destructive con ever.

I do not believe the lies of the meat delusion. I believe it is time to raise our voice in defence of truth, of justice, in the name of decency.

It is time to trash the most abysmal conspiracy in all of human history. It is time to annihilate the lies.

We can know the truth, we can think and act differently by thinking for ourselves, by challenging what we are told. When we dare to do so, we save lives. We can save ourselves from ourselves. We can save others from us. We can save the planet from humanity.

DARK SYMBOLS

Things are not what they seem. We are surrounded by corruption and wilful distortion. We are led to believe lies. It does seem, strangely, to be like something out of *The Matrix*, the 1990s sci-fi film about a synthetic world that hides the truth of what is really happening. One can either take the blue pill or the red pill, either stay in the fantasy or allow oneself to learn the truth.

What I call the meat delusion seems to work like this, whereby the violent, brutal and fatal confinement and killing of billions of sentient, sapient, pain-sensitive beings is taken as completely normal. Where the ingestion of the flesh of the slaughtered is taken for granted, and the drinking of the milk of female ruminants is seen as sensible and the consumption of embryos as a straightforward matter-of-fact daily routine. Where the felling of rainforests to grow grazing feed for livestock, the catching and killing of wild fishes to feed farmed fishes, the annihilation of mangrove swamps to make way for shrimp farms are all seen as economically and environmentally rational behaviours.

I am in a different place, it seems. I see things in a very different way. *The Matrix* concept of the fantasy world versus the real world has already been quite brilliantly applied to the livestock industry in the excellent animation, *The Meatrix*, but it extends far further than that, the fantasy reaching into every aspect of the social relationship between humans and non-humans. We do not see things for what they really are.

When I am in a supermarket and I see a slice of liver (for example) shrink-wrapped on the shelf, I do not see a consumer product, I do not see dinner or a meal ingredient. I see suffering and fear and I see pain and despair, and I see violence and cruelty. I see death. I see a body part. I see a part of a corpse. But others, so many all around me, seemingly so similar to me in every other respect, do not see any of those things, they seem to see a nice thing, something to be desired, and so into the shopping basket it goes.

When I see a carton on milk on the shelf, or watch an advert on television promoting dairy products, I do not see dairy products – I see yet more suffering and pain, I see illness and injury (fully half of the UK dairy herd at any one time suffers from mastitis, a very painful udder infection), I see disease (every pint of milk contains pus that leaked from those damaged udders), I see the despair of a mother lost without her newborn and I hear the bellowing of her desperate cries. I see the fear in the eyes of the newborn calf dragged from his mother and either shot in the head or trucked across the continent to suffer the brutal misery of a short, horrific life locked in a tiny crate to make "veal" – something regarded as a "delicacy", but I see no delicacy at all, I see cruelty and hateful violence against an infant animal.

I do not see what most people see. But I do know that the deaths of these animals are real, I do know that their suffering is real, that their cries and screams of despair are real, that the violence we inflict against them is real. I do know that the devastation of the land and marine environments is real, that the hunger agony of one billion people around the world is real and that it is real and true that fully half of all grain grown goes into the mouths of livestock animals. This is all real. I have taken the right pill. I do not live in a fantasy. I live in the real world and it breaks my heart.

Why are so many choosing not to know? Why do so many refuse to swallow the truth? Why are they more comfortable with and satisfied by violence and killing than compassion and caring?

The BBC's latest project to make entertainment out of the killing of other animals is a television programme called "*Kill It, Cut It, Use It*". Presented by Julia Bradbury, whom the BBC seems to want to use as the "poster girl" of the livestock industry (she also fronts "*Kill It, Cook It, Eat It*"), this programme is another twisting of the truth: non-human animals do not exist as mere tools for our use, are not mere objects of utility. It is not entertainment to show the violent destruction of a stressed, fearful, knowing being. And it is not moral to endorse that slaughter or regard it as "normal".

Compassion shows us how we can do things differently and how we can think differently. It takes courage to be compassionate in a world enslaved to cruelty but only compassion allows you to live in the real world.

SPEECH: ANIMALS COUNT CONFERENCE, 2010

Speech delivered to the Animals Count Spring Conference, in Islington (where I stood as their electoral candidate in the UK General Election 2010), 27 March 2010.

Today would have been the birthday of my mother-in-law Jennifer Kennedy, but she tragically died just before Christmas last year. Throughout her life she was a tireless defender of the rights of those who were browbeaten and downtrodden by our deliberately skewed and corrupt society, and as she was also a strongly loyal member of the Welsh community I think it is a fitting tribute to her on this day to open my speech with some fine words of a great Welshman, the poet and activist Raymond Williams, who said, "To be truly radical is to make hope possible, rather than despair convincing."

And following on from yet another recession, a Labour-inspired recession on this occasion to go with previous Conservative-driven collapses in the economy, and following on also from the dreadful failure of the Copenhagen Summit – the "last chance" to save the environment we were told – people now need to be given hope.

And so the task is set for us. We must make hope possible. We must be truly radical. Some may be concerned or worry about that, but they should not. For you see, to be truly radical we need do only one small thing – to tell the truth... To tell the truth about how so many of the ills that plague our human society have their roots in the way that we treat animals; to tell the truth about the reality of those animals' lives under our exploitation and how it is intolerable to allow it to continue; and to tell the truth about the profound significance of protecting our environment to secure a future for everyone.

And you know, it is remarkable to consider how much less daunting the challenge appears, and how much more possible and visible hope becomes, when you know that you have the truth on your side.

But still, let no-one doubt the measure of what is asked of us. There will be hostility to our proposals, there will be opposition to our call for change, there will be derision indeed in some quarters for our daring to even ask for what we want. And what do we want?

We want nothing less than to change an entire system. We know that a mere tinkering around the edges – as suggested by our major political parties – will not do; there is more, much more that we must do.

And so we make the call to *rethink* a whole philosophy that currently satisfies only a few at the expense of the many, and to *redirect* resources to those who need them most not to those who already have most and need more least of all, and we make the call to *reward* those whose contributions are currently unheralded, hidden and ignored, those who, for example, work in the caring, sharing professions, providing vital services to the powerless, the vulnerable and the dispossessed, and not to give even more reward to those whose work is socially useless and who flatter their own genius by conjuring ever more complex but utterly pointless and unnecessary financial structures that strain and burden the world with yet more debt.

So we make the call ... for real, radical change.

And there is no good reason why we should not. We have nothing to lose ourselves by telling the truth but everything to gain for those who need someone, anyone, to be honest on their behalf about what we are doing to them. I talk, of course, about the animals in our world, whether imprisoned in our farms and laboratories, or hemmed in, confined into ever smaller and ever more damaged habitats in the wild... wherever they are, they deserve someone to dare to be truly radical and to tell the truth on their behalf. Not because they have no voice of their own; they have a voice and they do use it when we cause them fear and suffering, but too many in our society have made themselves wilfully deaf to their cry of anguish, their scream of pain. Let us therefore raise our voice for them and make ourselves heard.

Some will say to us, "No, don't, it is not time", "The world is not ready to hear what you have to say", "Don't do it, you are asking for too much"... but the world is never ready for radical change, we could spend an eternity on the side-lines, as bystanders, idling away our years, patiently tapping our foot as we wait for the right moment to happen before we step out and ask meekly, "Is it okay now?"

No, we must be stronger than that. We should not shrink from nor shirk our responsibility to tell the truth *now*. It seems difficult, almost impossible even, but that is no reason at all not to do it. In fact, it is exactly the reason why we should do it. And history shows us why.

It may seem obvious and simple to us now, as though the whole world was in easy agreement with her, but when Mrs Emmeline Pankhurst stepped forward to challenge the outrageous misogyny of her age, a discrimination that brutally exploited the female half of this country's population, she was met with profound antagonism, hounded by her own Government, harassed by the forces of law and order, her liberty constantly under threat. Her call for change was a difficult call that was vehemently resisted by the powerful, but she made the call anyway. And she was right.

It may seem obvious and simple to us now, as though the whole world was stood behind her in fulsome support, but when Mrs Rosa Parks got on the bus in Montgomery, Alabama on 1 December 1955 and refused to give up her seat when told to but stayed sitting down where she was not supposed to, she was under the immense burden of legalised oppression, found herself under arrest and surrounded on all sides by open hostility. But she did what she did anyway. And she was right.

It may seem obvious and simple to us now, as though the whole world already knew that he would be a hero of our times, but when a young man, the Rev Dr Martin Luther King Jr. supported Rosa Parks in calling for an end to segregation, to put aside racial discrimination for all time, he was met with hysterical, intense and too often violent opposition. Millions of people hated everything he stood for and they hated him. His was not an easy journey, but he made the journey anyway. And he was right.

We are fortunate, then, that we can raise ourselves up onto the shoulders of these giants who were there before us, and be carried forward by their hard-won victories; we do not face the same dangers that confronted them, and we can learn from the message that they gave to the world – a message that says that the truth will out and the truth will win.

So, we can embrace hope and we can make hope the core of our message. We do not need to listen to, and in fact we can safely ignore, the doom-laden, scare-mongering lies of a Labour or Conservative administration. History has already decided on their incompetence, their impotence and their irrelevance.

We can already see, beyond the narrow, navel-gazing confines of what Labour or Conservatives would decide is good enough, that something more, a global hope for a better future, is being made possible, and we can share in this. We know that to think smart about what makes most sense for us here in the UK it is wise to look internationally, globally, to see what can be achieved.

When the Party for the Animals was established in The Netherlands and they first began their task of campaigning for election it was not at all obvious that they could gain genuine national prominence and electoral success, but that is what has happened, and in less than a decade they have achieved real political power, real political influence and they are making a difference.

In Bolivia next month, many thousands of delegates will assemble for the World Peoples' Conference on Climate Change, an event that will represent everyone's needs and interests in protecting our shared environment, and it will include the needs and interests of non-human animals.

And the Bolivian president, Evo Morales, has already succeeded in the adoption by the United Nations of an "International Mother Earth Day" and the first drafting of a "Universal Declaration of the Rights of Mother Earth", which includes the rights of non-human animals. One simply cannot imagine Brown, Cameron or Clegg showing such leadership as that. Let them, therefore, be only a benchmark for failure, and let them not be a standard for us and let them not represent us. We can do better than them.

And so we will. Our manifesto, our policies, our philosophy, together represent a practical and achievable proposal for a better world, a future in which everyone is entitled to their share, where the abundance created by our economy and the natural fruits of the Earth are shared fairly amongst all. We call for genuine partnership, collaboration and co-operation between all members of our community, and a genuine recognition and protection of those non-humans in our world whose personhood has been denied – against all scientific and moral evidence – for too long and whose rights therefore should be established in law and fully endorsed by a system of social justice that is all encompassing and all-embracing.

Our manifesto is a commitment to do better than obsess about economic growth at all costs, no matter what the cost to others, to do more than abdicate all responsibility to that perverse abstraction, "the market", which was claimed to be all-knowing and all-seeing but proved to be all wrong, and to demand more of our politicians than to yield and bow to the powerful and the pursuit of profit with no mind to the millions who are crushed underfoot in the race to the top.

Nearly 2,000 years ago a man called Jesus angrily threw out the moneylenders from the Temple, rather aggravated by their pernicious and corrupt influence. And how we may wish now that we had kept up that pressure on them!

Because today, the banks, really, are bankrupt, and the leeching, diseased parasite of free-market economics – that even now has its dark heart pumping the blood of bonuses around its festering form – is a system that is bankrupt too. But we know that the bank of justice is alive and well, and we will draw from its capital and make our call to rethink, redirect and reward, knowing that when we do so we can begin to restore a true sense of community and social togetherness and real hope for everyone.

The call that we make in our manifesto and in our campaign will resonate and echo down through the days, months and years to come, as a demand for a better society, a better world, a better future. This is what will give potency and the force to fight back to those who have feared, those who have lost hope, and it will answer the command of the as yet unborn narrator in Louis MacNeice's great poem, *Prayer Before Birth*, who pleads with us:

"... *fill me,*
with strength against those who would freeze my
humanity, would dragoon me into a lethal automaton,
would make me a cog in a machine, a thing with
one face, a thing, and against all those
who would dissipate my entirety"

So yes, we will. We will give people strength. We will be truly radical and we will make hope not only possible but utterly practical and achievable. Because it is time to bring democracy back to the people. We will stand in this election not only because it is our democratic right to do so, but also because it is absolutely right for us to do so. We speak for everyone and democracy must mean that everyone is heard, and so our voice is the voice of all in the community.

That is why we will use our voice in this election. We want to show that democracy is very much alive and kicking in this country, despite all that has happened; and we want to make it crystal clear that the major parties will not be unopposed – we will be there to challenge them; and we want to prove that the dispossessed, the disadvantaged and the downtrodden will have someone who will speak up for them, someone who will be a voice for the unheard, someone who will loudly make the call for justice for all.

Our task is set. To be truly radical, to make hope possible, and to tell the truth. And we will be a bulwark against the tyranny of lies with which we are daily assaulted. Nearly fifty years ago the late poet Adrian Mitchell was moved to fiercely denounce the corruptions and distortions by the politicians of his time when he wrote:

"you put you bombers in, you take your conscience out
you take the human being and you twist it all about
so chain my tongue with whisky
stuff my nose with garlic
coat my eyes with butter
stick my legs in plaster
tell me lies about Vietnam"

Well, half a century later and they're still lying. Our politicians lie about our involvement in illegal wars of aggression, they lie about the criminal use of torture, they even lie about which house they are living in; they lie about having to 'save the banks' with our money, they lie about the real cause of climate change, they lie about the failure of animal experiments, they lie about the abject lack of animal welfare on our farms, they lie about the damage done to human health by meat and dairy foods... they lie.

So we must tell the truth. And we will tell the truth. And we know where this treasure trove of hope, justice and truth is to be found – on the ballot paper, next to Animals Count, X marks the spot! So take every chance to tell everyone – vote for Animals Count: it's a vote for truth, a vote for hope, a vote for justice!

A VEGAN ON TOUR?

Written in early 2011 when there was much press coverage regarding the diet choice of professional cyclist David Zabriskie, who was due to take part in that year's Tour de France cycle race

There has been much press interest in the story that the American cyclist, David Zabriskie, is to race in the Tour de France on a vegan diet. As many people know, the Tour de France is one of sport's most punishing events, an endurance race that places unimaginable demands on the participants. It is famous precisely because it is so damned difficult, physically and mentally.

The reason that David Zabriskie's diet choice is creating such comment is that the ordinary expectation is that the sheer intensity of the race demands a very high calorie diet – most cyclists will consume an average of over 8,000 calories a day, three to four times the norm. It is considered normal to add huge amounts of extra protein to the diet on a daily basis, to help the cyclists recover from the exertions of the day's race and to prepare for the next day's strenuous schedule. This extra protein is pretty much taken in in the form of meat. Meat and more meat – that is the standard for a Tour de France competitor.

So the suggestion that someone can compete at all in the Tour de France on a vegan diet has surprised many. It's regarded as crazy, nonsense, just not the way to do it. But David Zabriskie swears by it and says that his performance has changed dramatically since the switch to the vegan diet – he says that he is in the form of his life, and did recently win a time trial during the Tour of California. His team members were initially wary of the dietary change but now say that no-one can argue with the results.

So a lot of people who normally wouldn't take any interest in the Tour will be watching closely to see how the vegan cyclist will fare.

There's just one problem though – David Zabriskie isn't a vegan and won't be on a vegan diet during the Tour de France.

David Zabriskie will be eating salmon fish twice a week throughout the duration of the tour. No-one who is a vegan eats any salmon fish ... ever... at all. One cannot be "mostly" vegan – either one is or one is not a vegan. Eating pieces of killed salmon fishes twice a week means that David Zabriskie is not a vegan and does not have a vegan diet.

It's like the classic question that comes up when one says to others, "I'm a vegetarian" and back comes the question, "Do you eat fish?" Sadly, I've known too many people who describe themselves as "vegetarians" but continue to eat fishes. That means that they are not vegetarians – they are meat-eaters who eat vegetables. This situation became so prevalent a few years ago that the *Vegetarian Society* in the UK felt compelled to produce little cards with pictures – a picture and definition of a fish on one side and a picture and definition of a carrot on the other side... just to help people to understand the difference between animals and vegetables.

It seems that we have the same problem now with being vegan – the consumption of animal-based foods is never an option for someone who is a vegan. There is no point and indeed it is both inaccurate and just plain wrong to describe someone as a vegan who even rarely eats animal-based foods.

It should be understood that to be vegan is not a mere diet choice (that may or may not be adhered to), it is not merely a lifestyle option – it is a way of life, a whole way of thinking and being that encompasses every aspect of one's life.

I know and understand that David Zabriskie has adopted what he describes as a "vegan" diet for purely dietary reasons – as far as he is concerned this has nothing whatsoever to do with animal welfare, or environmental concerns, it's only about performance in the world of professional cycling and to help him complete the Tour (he's failed to complete the Tour on two of the five occasions that he has taken part).

But we have to be clear – no vegan cyclist is taking part in the Tour de France 2011.

THE WITHDRAWAL METHOD II

Note: written on Wednesday 29 June, 2011 at the beginning the UK Government's "austerity programme"

On Thursday hundreds of thousands of public sector workers will go on strike in the UK. The strike is in protest at the Government's so-called "austerity measures", the pleasant-sounding phrase for the most dramatic cuts in public spending since the end of the Second World War. These massive public-spending cuts will severely impact on the quality of services that can be provided by these thousands of dedicated workers, adversely impacting on the living standards of millions of people and seriously harming future pension support for these workers when they retire.

The Government claims that there is no alternative, that these cuts must be enforced and that the public sector workers who are going on strike are "militant" and damaging "confidence". The Government has particularly emphasised those teachers who will be striking on Thursday, castigating them for their role in this day of action. The Education Minister, Michael Gove, has even suggested that parents can step in, by going into schools on Thursday to keep them open in the absence of many of the teachers. Quite what is to be achieved by non-qualified personnel "baby-sitting" pupils is not at all clear; certainly the parents will not be able to provide any formal teaching and how they are supposed to manage discipline issues or accidents is also anything but obvious.

But the intent is clear: to vilify teachers (and other public sector workers) for choosing to strike, declaring that it is "wrong" to strike, and that it is "wrong for the good of the country". Whilst the Prime

Minister, David Cameron, may claim that the pension system is "going broke" the National Audit Office has, in fact, already confirmed that the teacher's pension scheme is entirely affordable. But facts do not seem to matter. The Government is determined to press ahead with hugely damaging "reforms" that will harm the livelihoods of present and future public servants.

If this Government was truly interested in effective reform of the pensions system, and if the mantra "we're in this together" really meant anything, then they would have started a bit closer to home – with reform of the MP's pension system. But they chose not to. There has been and will be no reform of the absurdly generous pension arrangements that keep our politicians in luxury once they leave Parliament. Apparently, those arrangements are all fine and no reform is required. It is teachers and local government workers who are the problem and must bear the brunt of any fiscal changes.

Facts are irrelevant to this Government – they are hell-bent on trashing public services to ensure that profit is directed towards private companies who are given more and more control over an ever greater share of what should be our publicly-owned services. But privatisation, cuts to public services and deregulation of private finance have never improved the health of a national economy. They have massively increased the profits and wealth of the few at the top of society, but always at the expense of the many. What is happening in Greece right now is simply the situation in the UK writ large. The Greeks too are on strike.

The Greek public were not responsible for the nation's debts, and were not the cause of any imbalance in the economy. It is the banks in the UK, US and the Far East who are demanding the enormous repayments of their loans to the Greek Government, at extraordinary rates in such a punishingly short timeframe – demands that can only be met with yet more "austerity measures", yet more cuts to public services, more privatisation, cuts in wages, money for banks but not for education or healthcare.

So the Greeks, like their British counterparts on Thursday, are withdrawing their labour. And we must all support them. When jobs are threatened, when livelihoods are under such intense pressure, when wages are dropping through the floor but prices everywhere are going up, when the unelected business elite are able to keep their gold-plated pensions and award themselves astonishing pay awards year after year, and ever bigger bonuses year after year, when "negotiations" and "consultations" on your own pay and terms and conditions of employment lead to nothing, and your own Government turns against you, then withdrawing your labour is just about all that you have left. It is the one thing that they still need. Human labour is still the most valuable "commodity" or "resource" in any organisation. Refusing to labour for them is often the best that we can do.

So when these workers strike, even if we can't be with them in person, we can support them in spirit and in principle. We can refuse to believe the Government's lies and refuse to believe the lies peddled in the national press, which is now almost exclusively owned by big business interests and in no way speaks for the man and woman on the street.

I would rather that they did not have to strike, but I am glad that the workers are walking out, I am glad that thousands of schools will be closed... I am glad that someone is fighting back...

I'M NOT EATING THAT!

I was having a discussion about science and progress at work the other day and the conversation turned to artificial meat. This is meat that is grown from cells cultured in the laboratory and is not a "super" version of *Quorn* or other substitute for meat but the actual flesh product itself – grown in the lab. The same texture, the same consistency, the same composition ... not my cup of tea (or lunch or dinner!) of course, but this does represent a significant opportunity to eradicate the exploitation of animals for their body flesh.

Researchers are getting closer to being able to grow flesh in the laboratory and this would provide those who want to eat meat with the opportunity to do so without the requirement first to bring an animal life into being only for that animal to live a short, terrorised, desperately awful life before a brutal and violent killing. At a stroke, affordable and accessible artificial meat would eliminate the need for a "livestock industry".

Naturally, the flesh products that are grown would still have all of the health implications as with "real meat", such as being a cause of dietary cholesterol, but those who eat animal flesh today do so without obvious concern for their own health, and so this would not be an impediment to switching to lab-grown meat.

The research also shows that such cultured meat products would reduce greenhouse gas emissions by 96%! That is an extraordinary (and vital!) reduction and demonstrates very clearly just how damaging to the environment the livestock industry is at present. It would also free-up huge amounts of precious land and water currently taken by the livestock industry. The change for the planet (for the better!) would be immediate and dramatic.

So, such artificial meat would be better for animals (who would no longer need to be confined and slaughtered) and dramatically better for the planet... so what would stop people from eating it?

The answer is contained in the response from my meat-eating friend that I was discussing this with at work, "I'm not eating THAT!" (emphasis in the original!). He was horrified by the idea of eating something "made in the lab", and raised the spectre of "frankenfoods" and scientists "tinkering" with his food. The thought of what he "might be eating" was enough to put him off the very idea...

I also get this a lot with vegan food that is on the dinner table – very often "meaties" (can I call meat-eaters that?) will deliberately avoid the non-meat foods because they're "scared" of it. I remember at one party seeing a friend reaching out to grab a cocktail sausage, and I told him that it was a meat-free version, and then he pulled his hand away, and refused to eat any – he had more potatoes instead. He was really spooked by the idea. But it was just a soya-based product – what on earth did he think it would taste like? In fact, many months later, when he would eat such things, he agreed that the taste was absolutely fine and he really could not tell the difference... but it took him an awfully long time to come around to that way of thinking. Why the initial fear? Why the irrational reaction to something that is just meat free?

And, of course, meaties – including my work colleague who is horrified by lab-cultured products – are, it seems, more than happy to eat flesh from our farms and slaughterhouses, and we know only too well how appallingly filthy and disease-ridden are those places. The animals are confined in deliberately unsanitary conditions, with minimal veterinary care provided so wounds and sores go untreated; infection is rife and disease is endemic. Slaughterhouses, by their very nature, are astonishingly dirty, bloody places with bowel emissions running onto the "kill floor" along with blood and other body secretions, fouling the air and clinging to the meat with the slaughter of every animal.

Meat is filthy, faecal, riddled with bacterial infection and decaying from the moment that the animal is killed.

And people are happy to eat that? They really do eat THAT?

SURPRISED BY SURPRISE

The ethologist Jonathan Balcome was recently interviewed in The Guardian (the article appeared in July 2011) about his book "*The Exultant Ark: A Pictorial Tour of Animal Pleasure*". The Guardian writer says that it is "perhaps surprising" that "chickens recognise human beauty, starlings can be pessimistic and elephants grieve for their fallen comrades"... as illustrations from amongst many other examples of non-human animal emotions in Jonathan's excellent book.

I am always surprised that people are surprised that non-humans have emotions and feelings. Jonathan's book is a companion to his earlier work, "*Second Nature: the Inner Lives of Animals*", and his books are good companions to the great work done by the ethologist Marc Bekoff, eloquently expressed in his book "*The Emotional Lives of Animals: a Leading Scientist Explores Animal Joy, Sorrow, and Empathy and Why They Matter*" which again contains an abundance of documentary evidence regarding the complex psychological lives of non-humans.

In fact, we have an overwhelming, irrefutable mountain of data that demonstrate conclusively and dramatically that – of course – non-human animals have thoughts, emotions and feelings, just like human animals. They have brain systems, they have nervous systems, and they have sensory organs – why wouldn't they have emotions and feelings? It should be obvious that as species that have developed complex nervous and brain systems and the organ and sense ability to interact with their environment that they would naturally have the capacity to interpret that environment and have psychological and emotional responses to it. Why bother having a brain if it knows and feels nothing?

But still so many people deny the reality of non-human emotions and feelings, and act shocked and surprised when evidence emerges (yet again!) showing that yes, they do have emotions and feelings.

We know, of course, why this is. Because we treat those other animals so appallingly, because we mistreat them so violently, because we cause them so much injury ... and indeed death ... then we pretend that it's okay because they don't feel anything anyway. If we can convince ourselves that non-humans really are the "dumb" creatures that inhabit our fantasy world, and tell ourselves over and over that they're stupid, incapable of thinking, unable to think, too inadequate to feel, then when we confine them in tiny cages, force them to live lives in cramped, dirty and disgusting conditions, beat them, punch them, mutilate them, shock them, poison them and kill them ... it's all okay, no harm was done to anyone because they are not a someone, only an "it", an unthinking, unfeeling "it".

NO SMART GUYS IN THE ROOM

Note: written in 2011 when the economies of the Western nations were still reeling from the so-called "financial crisis" of 2008 that led to the collapse of some of the largest financial investment companies in the world and "required" the injection of vast sums of public money into private financial institutions to prevent further economic catastrophe

The current turmoil on the world's financial stock markets is symptomatic of the inherent failures in the world's global financial system. The intentions of the traders and bankers in their buying and selling on the world's markets are not based on any rational analysis of data but simply represent an irrational herd response to a "feeling". As one analyst put it, "Fear is the major theme." Billions, and indeed trillions, of dollars are being traded and trashed because of a feeling, a worry.

Too many of our media organisations gaze in awe at the financial markets, and bow in deference to the pronouncements of so-called market experts. But as someone who has worked in The City of London for 20 years, and spent many hours working with and drinking alongside traders and bankers from the major, global financial institutions, it is absolutely clear to me that we are not dealing with minds of great perceptive power and huge intelligence, the all-seeing and all-knowing seers of popular media imagination.

Despite the millions of pounds in fees that they can charge for their research, despite the millions of pounds that they can earn in salaries for their trading desk efforts, they really (and I mean this, they *really*) don't know anything more about how the economy works, or what is best for the economy, than what you do or I do, or even what a primary school-age child knows (more on that in a minute).

I remember being out having drinks with an investment banker from one of the banks I worked for during the early years of the century, and he was laughing and joking about how his research was just "nonsense, I make it up! But so long as it looks good, and the numbers look good, the clients just keep on paying me loads."

I also recall spending some weeks working with a banker from another investment house (a company that no longer exists, but was swallowed up by a competitor – an example of how capitalism will eat itself) on a Prospectus document for a new Internet-only financial news company for its IPO (Initial Public Offering – when a company begins trading shares on a stock market). This was a regular-sized Prospectus, around 250 pages, describing how this company would aggregate financial data from stock markets around the world and how it was great that this was "going to be on the Web" (this was back in 1999 at the height of the "dot com boom"). I remember being struck then that there were no "Financials" in the Prospectus. There was nothing, not a sentence let alone a paragraph or a section, about how this Internet start-up was ever going to make any money, ever. But it didn't matter. The investment house could still make millions in fees from investors who were desperate not to "miss out" on "getting into a dot com"; investor followed investor in pouring cash into a company that had no means, no mechanism, of ever making any ROI (return on investment). It folded a couple of years later, in the dot com bust, having never made any money, ever.

Some years later, and working for a different company, I remember supporting come colleagues on a series of documents called "securitisations" – packages of financial instruments that could then be sold to other investors, and sold again, and again. This time the documents were all about mortgages and I was surprised, even as a complete non-specialist on financial instruments, that these aggregations of mortgages were described as AAA-rated investments (the highest possible grade of investment). If it is one thing that every homeowner knows it is that one's home is at risk of being taken away if repayments are not made – which means of course that the potential is always there for a mortgagee to default on making those repayments! Therefore, I was completely puzzled as to how the brightest minds in some of the biggest finance houses and rating agencies could truly believe that bundles of mortgages represented the safest of investment opportunities! But the biggest banks on the planet spent years making huge profits (or *seeming* to make huge profits – the bonuses were real even if the profits weren't) out of selling and re-selling millions of mortgages. As we now know, this absurd mis-selling caused the biggest global financial crisis for over half a century: once people realised that the investments were basically junk, everyone panicked.

And that is just what happened as well in those silly dot com days. Someone panics, gets spooked and begins selling, and then everyone else thinks, "Whoah, why's he doing that? Damn, I'd better do it too" … and so it goes: fear, panic, no-one wanting to be seen not to be taking part (even if it means taking heavy losses), got to do what the guy next to me is doing [and it usually is blokes on the trading floor]. This mania follows the sun around the globe as the different markets trade during their day – the US followed by Asia followed by Europe, around and around, as the Earth revolves…

They don't know what they're doing and they don't know what to do next. These traders and investment bankers, as we know, get paid stupidly large sums of money for their alleged expertise, for their suggested deductive and analytical brilliance. They work in some of the best-maintained and finest working conditions of anyone on Earth (and kept spotlessly clean and shiny by large numbers of immigrant workers on the minimum wage). And yet they don't know anything more about how and where to invest than anyone else.

Many studies have been done over the years demonstrating – conclusively – that over a reasonable period, say not less than three or six months – a professional trader's decisions on which companies and which products to invest in perform no better on the stock market than the decisions made by a non-professional. There have been other studies involving the investment decisions of primary school-age children, who pick stocks based on "I like the name", or "my Dad's got one of those" and those children, on average, perform no worse than "professionals" paid millions of pounds or dollars. In some cases, they have outperformed the professionals and traded better.

So how do the traders get away with it? How come the non-professionals can't win? It's simple. The professionals have got unlimited funds to play with, whereas the little children or the non-professional trying to work as a day trader or just part-time, simply cannot compete for real, using real capital, real money; they can't do what the traders in their offices can do and continue gambling night and day, night and day, with no worry about funding limits.

The beauty of that of course (for the traders and bankers) is that the traders and investment bankers are not gambling with their own money – they're gambling with ours. If they make losses, big deal – they haven't lost anything, we have. It's where our pension funds disappear, our hopes for retirement that vanish – the traders are fine and they can just gamble again tomorrow, and the next day... they can trash an entire economy because of some irrational "fear" about what the economy is like (for example, Greece or Italy), or their irritation at Government expenditure on social provision for its citizens rather than investment in their client's financial instruments, or their anger at Government regulation on the gambling habits of banks, or their frustration at Government ownership of critical infrastructure (water provision, sanitation systems, energy) rather than "opening it all up" to free-market competition. With our money they can trash a nation. And then we pay for it, in reduced public services, more expensive energy and water, higher prices all round for the essentials for a decent standard of living.

People often look at other animals, social animals that live in herds, and see how they behave, all acting as one as the herd of sheep all turn in an arc on a hill, or the cows all move as one across the field, or perhaps they see a flock of starlings swoop and turn in one movement across the sky. People often think, "Stupid animals! Dumb creatures! Just following the herd! We're not like that!"

But they've got it wrong. The sheep, the cows, the starlings have all got perfectly good reasons I'm sure for making that turn, each following one another, and they do no harm. By contrast, the traders and bankers are painfully stupid, with their "He's doing it! I've got to do it!" attitudes and inability to even rationalise what the consequences are of their actions.

Let us be absolutely clear. The sheep and the cows and the starlings are a damned sight smarter than any trader or banker. Those animals wouldn't trash a nation, damage lives and ruin economies, just because of what the last guy said. They're not that bloody stupid.

MISSING THE (BLOODY) POINT

Note: written July 2011, prior to the execution of the pilot schemes for culling badgers that took place in the latter part of 2013.

There has once again been a lot of press and social media comment about a badger "cull" (mass-killing programme) in England and Wales, with the Environment Secretary, Caroline Spelman, saying that she is "strongly minded" to allow the shooting to death of badgers in the alleged attempt to prevent the spread of Bovine Tuberculosis (*bTB*). We should never forget, of course, that before entering Government Caroline Spelman had devoted her working life to lobbying on behalf of farmers and bio-technology firms so her position does not come as a surprise.

But even with making allowances for her deeply-biased background, Caroline Spelman's decision is ridiculous and absurd (as well as heartless and cruel) given that all of the scientific evidence indicates clearly and without equivocation that killing badgers is a pointless exercise in the control of *bTB*. Indeed, it is counter-productive and only exacerbates the problem of infection.

The real cause of the problem, of course, is the dairy industry itself. The overwhelming majority of *bTB* infections are caused by close contact between cows – *bTB*, obviously, is a respiratory disease and so an infected cow exhaling and coughing the bacteria into the aerosol environment in which other, non-infected cows are kept is the primary cause of herd infection. The dairy industry and supermarket retailers, however, in their demand for ever greater profit and with an ever-decreasing concern for animal welfare, are determined to crowd more and more cows into ever more confined conditions, and transporting them across country from farm to farm, further increasing the opportunity for infection between herds. They even want to confine these large animals inside huge sheds for the *entirety* of their lives to save money (so-called "zero-grazing" farming of ruminants). This, of course, is only ever likely to cause more stress to these animals, weakening their already damaged immune systems (because of their overwork in producing more and more milk), leading to more infections, more illness, more *bTB*.

But the farmers do not want to hear that they are the problem. They blame wildlife. They blame badgers. The farmers want to blame anyone else, any other species, anyone other than themselves for the problem, for the misery endured by these cows suffering from this desperate disease. And when they have shot all the badgers, and there is still *bTB* that is rife in the UK dairy herd, then the farmers will move onto some other species – it will always be the fault of someone else, never themselves.

The farmers do not want to believe that they are the problem and so they continue their obsession with shooting dead many thousands of badgers, wilfully ignoring the scientific evidence in the process. For them, the science does not matter, and because the farming industry has significant lobbying power with the Government then the Government too is prepared to disregard and discard the scientific evidence and proceed with the pointless, bloody slaughter of entirely innocent badgers. They are deliberately missing the point.

And there is one other group that is also missing the point completely. There are (inevitably!) many *Facebook* pages and *Twitter* accounts being set up to complain and protest about the badger killing because badgers are a protected species and lots of people *like* badgers. But many of those involved in these online campaigns also eat meat and dairy products. Everyone who pours cow's milk over a bowl of cereal in the morning or into their cup of tea or coffee is *directly* responsible and culpable for what is going to happen to the badgers. The badger cull is only going to happen to protect the interests of "livestock" farmers and they only have "livestock" in the first place because people want to eat the products they produce – the meat and dairy that are the remnants, the remains of these violated animals whose lives were short and brutal and whose deaths were violent and terrifying.

One cannot, legitimately, be aghast and horrified by the thought of badgers being shot to death but at the same time enjoy consuming meat and dairy products – those animals too are shot to death in the slaughterhouse (via a bolt fired into the brain) and suffer intensely and relentlessly during their brief lives to satisfy the demand for their flesh and other body products. It is a hypocrisy of the worst kind to protest against the one but not the other. As individual beings, the animals confined on our farms (cows) and the animals living wild next to the farms (badgers) are morally equivalent, and are therefore deserving of equal treatment and regard and respect.

The badger slaughter should not go ahead. That much is obvious. The meat and dairy industries too should not be allowed to happen. That much ought to be obvious as well...

THE GORE GORE GHOULS

I have something of a liking for gory horror movies and watched a great film the other day, "*Inside*", a French movie from 2009 starring Alysson Paradis and Beatrice Dalle. A genuinely very fine film, emotionally taut and deeply involving. There's also a heck of a lot of blood on show. I strongly recommend this movie. It lingers in the memory long after the final credits have rolled...

But I know that a lot of people won't watch it because it is violent; it does have a lot of blood being splattered everywhere. A lot of people just don't like that stuff. It's not a film for all the family. It's not uplifting, it's not a feel-good film... it is brutal and it is cruel. And a lot of people just don't like that. And I can understand that.

But what I can't understand is why many of those same people seem okay about the meat and dairy industries. If they don't like violence, and lots of blood being spilt, and don't like cruelty and brutality, why then do they like eating meat and dairy products?

At least with "*Inside*" I know that everybody's okay. At the end of the filming of those difficult, violent scenes the actors Alysson Paradis and Beatrice Dalle had a shower, cleaned off the fake blood, and went home. The studio hands got their buckets and sponges out and cleaned off the fake blood from the walls. The hammer and the knife didn't really cause injury, pain and extremely violent, bloody deaths... it was all pretend. Beatrice Dalle is a very good actress and a very nice person I'm sure – she doesn't really maim and kill. She wouldn't really do that for a living.

The slaughterhouse is real. The knives and the hammers really do kill. The people who work there really do maim, torture and kill for a living.

The walls are splattered with real blood; the channel on the "kill floor" runs very deep with a torrent of real blood. The workers' clothes are saturated in real blood, real scraps of split flesh, stained with the slashed mess of evisceration, the tissue of brain and spine. The slaughterhouse is truly hell on earth, an unceasing, unremitting, unyielding scream of violence, viciousness and cruelty. It is a totality of brutality. Mercy is dead at the gates. Within is only murder.

The slaughterhouse only exists because of those who want to consume meat and dairy products. The violence only happens because of those people. Those damned, bloody deaths only happen because of those people. The person who walks the supermarket aisle and picks up the meat and reaches for the carton of milk has directly, absolutely caused the bolt to be fired into the animal's head, has switched on the conveyor belt to take day-old baby chicks on a short, bewildering journey to the mincing machine, has spun the blade that slashes the throats, has powered the slicing blades that rip the animal's insides from his or her body, even as they breathe their last. The kill floor is awash with deep rivers of blood pouring from destroyed bodies that were only destroyed because of that person reaching out in that supermarket to do their weekly shopping. They made it happen.

The gore in the slaughterhouse is brutally real. An intense agony that never ends. No credits roll. No pretence, no fantasy, no "story", no joke.

People might not like my taste in movies but I can always honestly say that no-one was harmed in the creation of that entertainment but when someone sits down at table to enjoy their meat and dairy they absolutely cannot ever say that no-one was harmed. They caused harm. They killed. They may have washed their hands thoroughly before sitting down to eat but I can still see the stain of blood that lingers on their fingers and rings their mouth with every bite.

PAEDOPHAGIA – THE SICKNESS OF SOCIETY

They like them young. They like them very young. In fact, they love them young, and they love them very young. They want to get their hands on them when they're as young as possible. You can't describe them as youths, or even as juveniles really, because really they're just so very young, they're infants, they're just babies. That's all they are, just babies. Just babies and they want to get their hands on them, and get their mouths on them, just babies. You see their eyes light up, their hearts race, it really gets their juices flowing when they know they can get their hands on them and get their mouths on them, those babies. Just babies.

Older ones are not so good apparently, and old ones are just not of any interest at all. Not as much fun, not as exciting, it doesn't get them going in the same way, it's just not the same, they say. It's the young ones that they want, and it's the youngest ones of all that they want more than anything, as young as they can, to get their mouths on them and their hands on them.

The youngest ones are the best they say, that's what they tell me; I don't want to know but they tell me anyway, quite the glee and the delight in their voice when they talk excitedly – they really get quite animated a lot of them – when they tell me about the freshness, the smoothness of the youngest ones; it's the youngest ones – the babies – they're the ones, they love it, can't get enough of it, can't get enough of them, the babies, getting their hands and their mouths on the babies.

One is never enough. Can't just have one of them. More of them. More and more of them. Having another one and then another one, they can barely contain themselves to wait until the next one is born, get a bit of flesh on them and then they can get their hands on them and their mouths on them, and have them. It gets to be like an obsession it seems to me, though they would disagree with me, no doubt about it, they'd deny it, not obsessed at all, they don't need them at all, they just happen to like it, to like them, those infants, that's all, and they like having their hands and their mouths on them, it's just something they like, something they love, and love doing it, but it's not an obsession, it's just that they won't stop doing it. Why should they, they say to me, why stop it when they love it, when they want it, when they really enjoy doing it, and doing it to them, those babies?

What about the babies? That's what I say. Do they like it? Do you think they like what you do to them? That's what I say to them, and what they say to me is, oh, it's fine, I don't know why you're thinking of them even, it's perfectly natural, it's perfectly normal, to want to get your hands and your mouths on them, those babies.

They get quite defensive then, quite angry, quite offended that I've questioned them and asked them why they get their hands and their mouths on those little ones, those little undefended ones, the little infants, the babies. They don't like it, being attacked (as they see it) by me, being challenged about it because they like it, like doing it; they say lots of people do it, they know lots of other people who do it too, so why not do it, who am I – someone who doesn't do it – to tell them what to do, about doing it, about getting their hands and their mouths on the little ones? I don't even do it, so what the hell do I know about it? It's what they do, and it's what they want to do, and it's what they say they should do, that's what they say to me, quite defensively, in defence of what they do to babies. That's how they tell it. That's how they say it to me, when I ask them about what they do, with their hands and their mouths on the little ones, the littlest lives, the newest born, the babies.

Can I say it? Yes I can say it, and because I can say it I will say it – I hate it.

I don't like it and I have no choice but to say it – I despise it. I loathe what is done to the little ones, the babies.

I hate their pain, and I hate their suffering, I hate their violation and their destruction. I hate the way that we (no not I, but we as a society) corrupt them and kill them.

We – no not I – but we as a society, destroy baby animals by the millions. We bring them into life only to annihilate them. We drag them screaming from their mothers, in terror and fear as we violently pull them away, take them from their safety, their sanctuary, take them, crying and trembling from the warmth and the comfort, the gentle breath of their mother, from the soft touch of her skin, from the tender caress of her face, and we take them and haul them up onto lorries and lock them into tiny cages. We brand their newborn bodies, the stain of slaughter, they're ours now, and the mother bellows and cries for her son and her daughter but we ignore her because the little ones are ours now, not hers. To hell with the mother, damn her, we've got the baby now, the baby now is ours, for us, just for us, only for us to get our hands on and get our mouths on. We love it.

No, not we, certainly not I. I don't love it. Who loves it? Who is it that loves it? Who loves getting their hands and their mouths on babies, who is it who loves eating babies? I don't get it, I just don't get it. Who'd like it, to eat babies? How can anyone like it? How can anyone love being a paedophagic, how can anyone be happy to be a paedophagic, how can anyone get off on being a paedophagic? How can they even like it and not deny it and be proud of it? How can anyone like getting their hands and their mouths on the cut up bodies of violently slaughtered baby animals?

How does anyone do it and not mind it? But they really do it, and they do it a lot. 15 million lambs brutally killed every year in the UK – not more than four months old (and they could live to be 15 years old!) and many only a couple of months old, just around ten weeks of age. Just babies. Tiny offspring to gentle mothers left shocked and crushed by the loss of their newborn. A couple of months old, barely time to learn to leap and play, and yet trucked to a violent, terrifying slaughter in the abattoir.

Just babies. And then I see it. The paedophagic's fattened, reddened cheek bulging, the diced cut of flesh squashed between jaws, chewed and chomped on as the mouth upturns into a grin of delight – ooh, that's nice – and the eyes are alight with pleasure – oh yes, that's good – and the neck swells with a swallow. Oh yes, oh yes, I liked that, god I liked that. A self-satisfied silent burp, the burst of air from the expanding gut that digests the leg of a lamb who screamed in horror and in pain, shook in terror and in fear, and who looked desperately for her mother, and tried to hide, tried to get away, but the man wanted her, wanted her dead, and so even though she had only a tiny flash of time, just a tiny moment of time to feel the sun on her face, the wind through her fleece, the call of her mother in her ears, just a tiny flash, well now that's gone, done, and so she is dead, done to death, just so the ones who love to get their hands and their mouths on babies can get it and have it and love it. Oh yes, that's nice, loved it, they say, that was good. How satisfying for them.

I am sickened by society. Society is sick. It is a disgusting horror of a twisted, sick world with paedophagics down every street, on every damned corner, openly strutting their stuff in every town and city, on the lookout for yet another one to get their hands on. And they get their pleasure; the paedophagics get their babies, they get their hands and their mouths on the bodies of babies.

It makes my skin crawl and worst of all is that our society endorses and sanctions and supports these paedophagics, gives them everything they want and indulges their every desire, and those who profit from selling babies' bodies get subsidised for doing it, for selling bodies, for selling babies to death, the government gives them money to let them carry on doing it because so many people want it, they love it, getting their hands and their mouths on the bodies of dead baby animals.

There is a sickness in society, an epidemic of paedophagia, and it stalks my waking moments and it haunts my sleeping moments, and it gives me no rest and no peace, and I will have no rest and no peace and I want no rest until I rid this world of its sickness, of the sufferance of the innocent, until the babies are left to live, are left to live and grow, to play and to run, to love their mother and be loved by their mother, to be left close to their mother to learn and to grow and to live. I will not rest and I do not want to rest until every last one of them, the little ones, the littlest ones, those babies, are left alone to live, until they're all left alone to live…

Note: and of course it's not only lambs, it's also the pigs who are killed at just five or six months of age, the chickens who are killed at around just six weeks of age, the turkeys killed at just three to six months of age, and so on and so on and so on, millions and millions of babies, hundreds of millions, all babies, just babies…

SPEECH: WORLD DAY FOR ANIMALS IN LABORATORIES, 2010

This is the text of the speech that I gave at the national World Day for Animals in Laboratories demonstration in London, 24 April, 2010.

I was here last year on this march, a fine and sunny day then as well, and I gave a speech on that occasion too. But I would really like not to be here next year, because like you I would really like to see an end to these marches because like you I would really like to see an end to the horror of animal experimentation.

And so, whilst on the one hand it is great to see so many here today, on the other it is sad of course that we are here at all, for we know we are here only because today so many others are imprisoned, in pain and at the mercy of those who would kill them, simply to satisfy their curiosity, safeguard their academic prestige or protect and maximise their profits and the money in their pockets. In other words, for no good reason at all.

As the Parliamentary Candidate for Animals Count in the General Election, I am going out to the electorate every day, I am engaging in debate with our elected representatives and I am making the call for justice for all, and unlike all of those other politicians, I really mean it!

Animals Count demand an immediate end to the unjustifiable, intolerable harm done to those millions confined in the UK's laboratories. We know that justice can only be served if enslavement is eradicated everywhere, and that must include putting an end to the violent incarceration of animals in the UK's research institutions.

The science is so very clear and I do not need to repeat the detail of that which we already know, but I can restate simply that to take a healthy animal who has the potential to live a rich, fulfilling life and to imprison and then by design to fatally poison or mutilate him or her is a moral outrage, an affront to decency and an abomination of science. It is nothing less than the calculated corruption of the scientific method and its support requires nothing less than the deliberate distortion of the data and the wilful misrepresentation of the evidence...

Over time science should represent progress, a process of adapting to the accumulation of evidence that most effectively fits the results of experiment. But the so-called "science" of vivisection is stuck in a backward time, a dark-age relic of discredited methods and data, a fossilised failure that should be forgotten and discarded in the shadow of its shameful history.

Were the science of astronomy to act in so backward a fashion then we would still believe that the sun revolves around the Earth, and dismiss the mountain of evidence to the contrary as a mere irrelevance. Were the science of geography to act in so backward a fashion, we would be still be fearful of falling off the edge of the world lest we stray too far from land, and dismiss the mountain of evidence to the contrary as a mere irrelevance.

But fortunately these sciences mature and they recognise that good science is self-correcting and adapts and adjusts to the abundance of evidence. And so it is time for all sciences to do the same and follow the evidence and not the pursuit of profit at all costs, no matter what the costs to others. It is time to do away for all time with the intellectually inept and dishonest nonsense of vivisection.

We can be honest – we know that there a lot of very bright people working in those laboratories, they are dead smart. But as the late Carl Sagan was fond of saying, "Being dead smart is no guarantee against being dead wrong." And so we must free those bright minds from the darkness of that dishonest science. We should protect our academics from the pressures and coercion of profit-driven industry, and free our young scientists from the pernicious influence of their professors who are too often determined only to hold onto old ways. Medical science can flourish wonderfully and our finest minds can soar with the creative possibility that comes with opening up to progress and not having to hide in fear from the harassment of global business.

But we also know that ultimately it really isn't about them, it is about those others, locked behind bars in torturous confinement and unremitting misery, in deep and unending despair and pain. They remain our absolute, direct moral focus in our determination to see an end at last to that corrupt and corrupting system that debases science, fails our scientists, and causes such appalling suffering and agony.

But we can know this – it's been a long time coming, but a change is gonna come.

I can tell you this: we are a very fortunate generation; we are favoured by history, because we are the ones who will see the world change. Our time is at hand.

So even though I know that our hearts are heavy on this, another dark day in many ways despite the sunshine, when we know so many are suffering, we can have hope in our hearts. Because I know that when the tide of history turns, it turns with us. Our time is at hand. It is our truth that will let loose a torrent that will flood the foundations of that false science and bring the walls of oppression crashing down. Our time is at hand.

We will see the day when men and women from across the biological and medical sciences meet together in conversation with us and they say to us, "We know the truth and it has set everyone free! It has set us free from days of maiming and killing, it has set our patients free, left abandoned to their fate with pills that did not work, and it has set all of those animals free... from misery, imprisonment and pain." We will see the day!

We will see the day when the instruments of torture and killing are melted down, broken down and recycled, re-made into new materials, materials that support not death but life... we will see the day!

And we will see the day when we can walk lawfully into the last of those research labs, and we will be there when the last cage door is opened and we will see as the last animal is carried gently forward from confinement to everlasting freedom... we will see the day!

THE RISE AND RISE OF SANITISED VIOLENCE

The release of data that show that the number of animal-based experiments in the UK has risen again comes as no surprise. The number of animals abused in such experiments has been on a steady upward curve for many years (after a slight dip during the 1980s and early 1990s).

Millions of animals die painfully every year in UK laboratories. The lie is still propagated that such experiments are "essential" for medical progress and "critical" to improve human health. This is a brutal and cruel lie. Anyone who doubts the failure of animal-based research would be advised to read Dr Andrew Knight's excellent and vital study, *"The Costs and Benefits of Animal Experiments"*, bringing together a decade's worth of research.

The same day that these figures were released regarding animal experiments there was the release of some other statistics from the Macmillan Cancer Support charity, indicating that four out of every 10 UK citizens will develop cancer at some stage in their lives. As far as many people are concerned, fear of cancer is coupled with the demand for more research – research that is more often than not animal-based. People generally believe, and are led to believe, that animal experiments are essential to seek cures for diseases that terrify the general public – including cancer, Parkinson's and Alzheimer's.

Therefore, as far as most people are concerned, without those animal experiments there will never be a cure for those devastating diseases. It is not, though, the "average" man or woman in the street who chooses to make this connection between human diseases and animal experiments – this is something that they are told by senior medical professionals and the Government. People believe that these highly-paid, highly-experienced and highly-qualified personnel must know what they are talking about, and so there is no need to question what they are saying. So, everyone agrees – to cure humans of disease we must experiment on non-human animals.

This is an absurd and brutal, vicious lie. Here is one reason why: advocating for more animal experiments, Prof Roger Morris argues "...real diseases are diseases of the whole body, and can only be studied in the whole body. To take the example of Parkinson's – a disease that is very common and devastating. Part of this disease is a dopamine deficiency in the neurons, but the underlying cause is a complex set of interactive problems, that probably involves an inflammatory or autoimmune component... we can't study that in tissue culture of individual cells."

Here's the problem: human beings are the only primate that suffers from Parkinson's disease. No other primate experiences this condition. And so the non-human primate research into Parkinson's disease that is conducted involves invasive surgery to cause immediate, massive brain trauma that will mimic (ie, not be the same as) some of (but never all of) the kinds of symptoms seen in a human being suffering from Parkinson's. The primates are then experimented upon with a battery of drug treatments before being fast-tracked to death so that the experimenters can access and examine their brains and nervous system. In humans, of course, Parkinson's is a slow-acting, progressive neurodegenerative disorder causing loss of motor and other function over a long period of time.

In other words, what happens naturally to human primates, and what the experimenters cause to happen to non-human primates, are totally different. They are not studying the same disease. Indeed, with the non-human primates it isn't even a "disease" – it's deliberately inflicted brain damage.

So, whilst Professor Morris may suggest that researchers need to study "the whole body" (and not merely tissue cultures), with regards to Parkinson's they are studying the *wrong* body! All that the research tells us is what happens to non-humans when their brains are deliberately mutilated; it tells us nothing about how the disease occurs or advances in humans.

A vile, pointless waste of time, money and lives – both non-human primate lives, and human lives. A most appalling deceit is pedalled to sufferers of Parkinson's and their families who are promised false hope that this research can help them. How cruel. How despicable.

The same is true of other human diseases including cancer which looms so large as a spectre that haunts the mind: no-one wants to suffer cancer or for their loved ones to be so diagnosed. But cancer in humans is not the same as cancer in other animals, still less the rodents who are most usually experimented upon in cancer research. The response of mice to cancer treatments is a very poor predictor of how humans respond to precisely those same treatments and medications. Causing cancer in mice and then treating them tells us nothing about cancer in humans. It tells us about cancer in mice. Once again, the researchers are looking at the wrong body!

Time and again the promise is made of a great breakthrough in seeking a cure for such awful diseases, and this makes for great headlines in the media; yet again the adverts appear on television asking for donations to do more research. But over and over again the treatments and the drugs fail when given to people, and this never makes for any headlines in the media. No-one wants to tell the truth about the failure of "successful" animal experiments...

The researchers are always looking in the wrong place, looking at the wrong body, looking at the wrong physical "system"... analogously this is similar to having a major, critical error with a computer's Windows 7 operating system (a not unknown phenomenon!) but then going to an FAQ website for the Unix operating system to find out what's going wrong, or having engine trouble with a jet aircraft and picking up the manual for a motorbike to figure out how to fix it... perhaps you are in Paris, on holiday, and can't make out what the waiter is saying to you in French and so you refer to a Hebrew phrasebook for the answers...

In each of these cases there are similarities (operating systems have file stores, aircraft and motorbikes have engines, French and Hebrew languages both have verbs and tenses), and indeed many similarities, but there are also differences, and the differences are absolutely crucial. It matters what you're looking at. In the case of medical research, it matters *who* you're looking it.

It's just wrong. It is just plain wrong. Either the experimenters do not know the difference between humans and non-humans (in which case, they really shouldn't be let loose in a laboratory) or they do know the difference – in which case they are immoral and brutal to the deepest degree.

SUMMER FUN

The bull-running season in Spain is in full-swing. We read today (*this was written on 15 August, 2011*) of one bull who has now killed a man for the third time. This was a senseless and pathetic death, the sheer idiocy of the man who died cannot be over-estimated, and neither can the monumental arrogance, ignorance and cruelty of the crowds participating in these festivities. One feels so sad for Rotan, the bull used in this particular festival. He is deeply traumatised, shocked and terrified by the experiences he is forced to endure, all for the supposed entertainment of others. The harm we do to him, and so many others like him, is indefensible and despicable.

Many in the UK are – rightly – horrified by the bull-running spectacle in Spain. But we cannot claim any moral advantage from our position here in the United Kingdom. Last week, 12 August, marked the start of the shooting season when people take their guns to the fields and moors in the countryside to shoot birds from the sky. Killing for fun. What a way to spend an afternoon.

It is claimed that this is about "conservation" but we know that Mother Nature does not need a helping hand to manage her natural environment from someone with a gun. We do not need people whose job titles are "gamekeepers", whose lives revolve around the exploitation and killing of other animals. "Game-keeping" is typical of the human and non-human relationship: it is about cruelty, brutality, violence and killing. Killing and more killing, over and over again.

I can sit outside and admire the sun, the warmth of its rays, and wander fields and hills and admire the grasses and the other lives I come across whether land-living or flying on the wind. I can be amongst the natural world and be amazed and awed by its complexity and magnificence, and I can do that without once feeling the need to kill anyone.

I do not have to kill and I do not want to kill. I do not have to taunt and mock an already frightened, terrified animal just to have some fun at a festival, and I do not have to take a lethal weapon and discharge its violence towards those soar so magnificently in the sky. I do not have to and I do not want to. And no-one else *has* to kill either, no-one else *needs* to kill, and it is morally sick if anyone *wants* to kill.

To think that we cannot have festivities without killing is a massive failure of imagination, wit and intelligence. To think that nature needs to be "managed" and her offspring need to be shot to death is ignorant and plain stupid.

Our pleasure, our fun, cannot come at the expense of the safety, comfort and lives of those others with whom we share this world. If we truly believe ourselves to be the "best" species (whatever that means!) then surely we can have the creativity and wisdom to act only in a manner that does not cause trauma, stress and death. Fun does not have to be blood red with violence.

It's a beautiful day today, and the sun looks glorious against a soft blue sky... but I wish that today was not a fatal day for those beautiful others...

To live well is surely to love life... and to love life is surely to love and care for *all* lives.

SPEECH: WORLD DAY FOR FARMED ANIMALS, LONDON, 2010

This is the text of the speech that I gave at the World Day for Farmed Animals, central London, 2 October 2010.

*"Cursed are dullards whom no cannon stuns,
That they should be as stones.
Wretched are they, and mean with paucity
that never was simplicity.
By choice they made themselves immune
To pity and whatever mourns in man"*

Those words were written by Wilfred Owen in his great poem, *Insensibility*, about the First World War, and he was compelled to write those words because he was shocked, shaken and appalled that people "back home" in the UK were utterly unmoved by the carnage, the horror, and the waste of the war on the Western Front... this jarring fact was for Mr Owen nothing less than the debasement of humanity.

And now, in a very different situation but for a very similar reason must I state the stark, bloody fact that, by choice, the meat and dairy "consumers" in our society have made themselves immune to all of the extreme, vile violence done daily to millions of non-humans in their name and for the sake of mere profit and pleasure. To satisfy the desire for a bite to eat, a burger or a sausage or two or a splash of milk in a cup of tea, people choose to remain as dullards, as stones, in the face of the cry of agony – they have no pity.

Well I choose too. And my choice is to raise my voice and to stand opposed to those who remain immune to the suffering of the innocent, the defenceless; those animals who are utterly at our mercy and are shown no mercy or pity but instead get a kick in the face and a knife in the throat. No-one should sanction and be satisfied with the horror of the farm and the slaughterhouse.

But many are satisfied, and they are satisfied because they have allowed themselves to be lulled and pacified by a soothing, calming, cosy lie – it's all okay because we must eat meat, apparently, even though I eat none of it and I haven't died, and you eat none of it and you haven't died. But it's all okay because – well, why should we care? After all, they are only animals.

The common opinion says that farmed animals are all stupid, they have no understanding of the world, they are unthinking, unfeeling, and unknowing, are but beasts, dumb, with no language, no emotion, no mind, and thus there is no need, no need at all, for us to care for their welfare or their lives and deaths.

Thus, we may commit violence against them; we may confine them; we may beat them, kick them, hit them; we may poison, burn, cut, mutilate, stab them as we want. We can tether and tie them, deny them any freedom of movement, refuse them food, water, living space, the chance to breed, the chance to nest, burrow, fly, forage – whatever would be their alleged "want" we can remove it and replace it with a chain and a cage. We can make them die when and how we want them to. And whatever we do to them, and we can do anything we want to them, we do not have to care about it being done, we need never give thought or consideration to what happens to them under our hand, under our boot, under our knife; however much the blood flows, or a cry emerges from the mouth, however much the "beast" may struggle, twist and turn to run, however much it may seem as though the "brute" reacts to our rough handling and violent killing, it only seems to be so, it is not really so, it is only a "seeming", it is not real because they are not real, they are not a "they" but a mere "it", so kill it, cook it, eat it, just a thing, a thing with no more mind than an up-ended rubbish bin, they do not think, therefore they are not, they are only nothing ... ... and that, all of that, is a bright, shining, murderous lie.

To believe that it does not matter, to believe that it is "no big deal" that these animals suffer terribly in fear, to believe that it is okay for it to be so because they are "only an animal" is to fall into a foul conceit, shielding one's mind to an obvious truth, retreating into a fantasy utterly disconnected from the real world, smothering oneself in a comforting blanket of lies. The suffering, fear, despair, pain, terror endured and experienced by any bull, any cow, any sheep or chicken is every bit as real, as viscerally, dramatically, appallingly real as the fear and despair of any human... and if it is just plain wrong to cause any human to endure fear and pain, the desperate horror of incarceration, torture and the terror of an imminent, bloody death then it is just plain wrong to cause these farmed animals that life-long misery and horrific death too.

To deny the richness, variety and depth of non-human animal experience is to deliberately lie about everything that is visibly, obviously on display whenever we encounter a farmed animal. Their senses are finely tuned to the environment around them, in many cases more finely tuned than our own, offering a richer appreciation and awareness of the natural world than any human ever could. It is absurd to believe that they have in any way a "weaker" experience of their environment than us. It is different, yes, but not in any reasonable sense, "weaker". Their world and their life matter to them. They should matter to us too.

Countless stories attest to the vast range of farmed animal emotions, their cognitive abilities, their interpretive analysis of the outside world and the full measure of their psychological and emotional comprehension of what is happening to them, good and bad. The animals that we farm know what we are doing to them, and they do not like it. The animals that we farm understand their fate and they are desperate to avoid it. The animals that we farm look into our eyes, see our intent, and they are terrified by it.

But today is the day when we can stand proud in our determination to recognise them and acknowledge them and respect them, and so –

> to the exhausted cow barely recovered from childbirth, worn and tired, and in desperate sorrow bellowing for her lost calf, stolen from her,
>
> > we know you and we will remember you
>
> to the disabled chicken with broken wing and burned feet, crippled and unable to stand, barely emerging from infancy, only a few weeks old and already destined for a bloody death,
>
> > we know you and we will remember you
>
> to the bull who is heaved up, hanging upside down from the hoof, bruised and beaten, seeing, hearing, smelling the killing of his cousins,
>
> > we know you and we will remember you
>
> to the male chick discarded like rubbish into a refuse sack, weighed down and crushed by his brothers, unable to breathe and slowly dying,
>
> > we know you and we will remember you

to the sheep who peeps her head from the side of the truck taking her to her killing, reaching, grasping for a final gasp of fresher, life-giving air,

we know you and we will remember you.

Like you, I carry their pain in my heart and the moral horror of what is done to them through my every waking hour.

We know that we cannot stop it all today, and heaven knows we know we cannot stop it all tomorrow, and we cannot save them all today and we cannot save them all tomorrow but like you, I will never sway in my resolution and I will never waver in my opposition to this industry of carnage and cruelty, this most barbarous and pathetically pointless of humanity's murderous schemes, and I will absolutely will not stop – ever – until that damned industry is done for and damned to history for all time and we see the rising of the sun on that glorious day when we can finally say, "They're free today, they're all free today, everyone last one of them is free today!"

YESTERDAY

"We have learned from the past
And now we are wise
Just so we can eat
No-one else dies"

We confined all the animals
And we tied them all up
We ripped open their throats
Then we cut them all up

We burned their bodies
And we called it meat
And that is the way
That we used to eat

But that was yesterday
And today is today
And all we have now
Is tomorrow
Goodbye and to hell
with all the ways
of those damned yesterdays

We trapped all the cows
And then we raped them
We killed all their babies
And then we ate them

We fondled the teats
And drank it all up

And that is the way
That we used to sup

But that was yesterday
And today is today
And all we have now
Is tomorrow
Goodbye and to hell
with all the ways
of those damned yesterdays

In early spring
The lambs were born
We let them run free
In the sun to be warm

Then we dragged them away
And we cut open their throats
We killed all those babies
To keep our business afloat

But that was yesterday
And today is today
And all we have now
Is tomorrow
Goodbye and to hell
with all the ways
of those damned yesterdays

The chickens we kept
Cooped up in those sheds

We'd cut off their beaks
And cut off their heads

The males that got born
Would never give eggs
So we sliced them to death
We thought they were dregs

But that was yesterday
And today is today
And all we have now
Is tomorrow
Goodbye and to hell
with all the ways
of those damned yesterdays

We got in our boats
And went out to the sea
Scooped up all the fishes
'Till none were left free

We stamped on their heads
And sliced open their gills
Bleeding to death
For our dinnertime thrills

But that was yesterday
And today is today
And all we have now
Is tomorrow
Goodbye and to hell

with all the ways
of those damned yesterdays

Those who ate this stuff
All of them got sick
They begged their doctor
Please heal me quick

Their bodies were messed
All riddled with cancer
They thought popping pills
Was the only answer

Their hearts gave out
All clogged up with crap
But they kept on with the meat
They'd never cut that

So the graveyards were full
With those that died
Because they ate those
Whose bodies they fried

But that was yesterday
And today is today
And all we have now
Is tomorrow
Goodbye and to hell
with all the ways
of those damned yesterdays

LIKE ANIMALS?

Note: written in August 2011 when England was gripped by a week of street violence and rioting

With all of the rioting that has been taking place in the UK, much of the commentary has obviously centered on the behaviour of the rioters. The terms used to describe them are what one would typically expect – "feral", "like animals", "animalistic", "roaming like a pack of animals".

The problem, of course, with these descriptors is that the analogy implied – that these youths are behaving like animals – is invalid. Non-human animals do not behave in such a way as to cause wanton destruction, violence and trashing of their local environment. The behaviours exhibited by the rioters are uniquely human – only our own species indulges in such truly mindless, pointless destructiveness, only we humans set out with the intent to cause mayhem and violence for its own sake.

Some animal species (for example dogs or wolves) may roam in packs, but this is a perfectly natural behaviour for their kind and it serves an explicit purpose, to help the pack members to hunt, acquire food and keep safe in a hostile world. For such pack animals this is a critically important survival strategy.

We cannot say the same about the human rioters, merely looking out for a new pair of shoes or mobile phone. Neither the shoes nor the phone were a necessity in the sense that the rioters' survival depended upon their acquisition; I bet that none were without any footwear of any kind and no technological means of engaging meaningfully in society (much was made of the fact that some riots were organised by BBM (Blackberry Messenger)). Many millions of people in the Majority

World are in exactly that position, but these riots took place in what is described as the "First World" where footwear and the "latest tech" are much more readily available.

The main point of course is that non-human animals do not commit wanton violence – only we do, and it is a desperate lie (as well as being deeply unfair) to describe these violent youths as being in any way "like animals". They are animals of course – in the sense that they are members of the animal kingdom, but their behaviour and their intention to destroy for its own sake are uniquely human characteristics.

This is not a petty or trivial point; I am not simply trying to be "politically correct". The language and phrasing that we use daily has important implications for how we regard others; the labels that we apply to others have consequences for how society treats them. It is because society generally uses and thinks of the term "animal" in exclusively negative terms, as something base, primitive, unworthy, that we treat non-human animals with cruelty and violence and disregard their interests and ignore their suffering.

Which is, of course, the other side of the riots issue. Much of the commentary has described how the violence and property destruction has been "pointless", "pure thuggery", "unthinking", "wholly unnecessary". People are outraged, appalled, shocked and horrified by the committal of pointless violence...

And yet so many of those same appalled, outraged people will still happily tuck into their plates of meat. They are happy to indulge the meat industry, and will most likely eat meat on a daily basis. But we know that to have meat means that one must first violently put to death a sentient, sapient, pain-sensitive, fearful individual animal. We know too that one can live perfectly healthily without any animal-based foods at all. Surely, therefore, it logically follows that meat production represents the most reprehensible, most pointless expression of violence.

Why is no-one outraged by the violence in the slaughterhouse? We know the cruelties and horrors that are the minute-by-minute terrors endured by those pained, deeply distressed animals. And we do nothing about it.

People want to pick and choose the acts that will cause them outrage, speaking out loudly on some but remaining perfectly silent on others. But that, of course, is no way to live – that does not represent living an ethical, moral life.

If pointless violence is an outrage then it is an outrage in *every* case, and that must include the brutality on our farms and slaughterhouses.

A MASSACRE BY ANY OTHER NAME

Written following comments made by the singer Morrissey (previously of The Smiths) onstage at a concert in Warsaw in July 2011, shortly after a mass killing of students in Norway.

Many will by now be familiar with the controversy over the singer Morrissey's remarks on stage in Warsaw suggesting that the murder of dozens of young people in Norway was "nothing compared to McDonald's and KFC." There was immediate outrage from many that Morrissey had dared to compare the killing of these young people with the daily killing of farmed animals, including outrage from many in the audience, who ought at least to have understood Morrissey's uncompromising stance on these issues. After making the remarks, Morrissey launched into The Smiths' song, "Meat is Murder".

Morrissey has since defended his onstage comments, by explaining further that:

"The comment I made onstage at Warsaw could be further explained this way: millions of beings are routinely murdered every single day in order to fund profits for McDonald's and KFCruelty, but because these murders are protected by laws, we are asked to feel indifferent about the killings, and to not even dare question them. If you quite rightly feel horrified at the Norway killings, then it surely naturally follows that you feel horror at the murder of ANY innocent being. You cannot ignore animal suffering simply because animals 'are not us'."

Morrissey makes an extremely trenchant and important point. At no time was he trying to disparage or mock or make light of the horrific, vile, pointless and brutal slaughter of those dozens of innocent young people in Norway, lives destroyed in their prime, simply because of one man's belief system, warped and twisted as it is. But what he was doing was making explicit the fact that our society is complicit in the daily slaughter of millions of innocent (and most often young) non-human animals, lives destroyed in their prime (broiler chickens are just 42 days old at slaughter; pigs just six months old), simply because of our belief system – that we "must" eat meat to be healthy and to survive. This is as warped and twisted a belief system as any.

We know, the evidence is beyond challenge, that we do not need to eat meat to survive or to be healthy, and indeed the evidence demonstrates that one can easily survive and be healthier if one removes meat from the diet. To want to have meat therefore is a want that is based not on necessity but on mere belief, an opinion that does not withstand the evidence of science.

To support the fallacious opinion that meat is essential, billions of innocent, pain-sensitive, sentient and sapient beings are brutally put to death in the cruellest manner that we can devise. The recent video evidence released by the campaigning group *Animal Aid* showing the violence and viciousness meted out to pigs in a slaughterhouse (Cheale Meats) in Essex, England is but the latest of many examples of how appallingly we destroy the lives of farmed animals. Examples of the brutality include stubbing out cigarettes on pigs' faces, punching them, and firing electric tongs on a pig's face and anus.

There will be no prosecution of the workers filmed committing these acts because (as DEFRA have stated) the evidence was "based on CCTV footage gained without the consent of the relevant Food Business Operator". A highly specious reason indeed. The BBC recently filmed undercover at a care home and obtained secret video footage of abuse by staff of the residents and prosecutions have swiftly followed – the video evidence was obtained without the consent of the care home owners. The distinction being made in this case is that *Animal Aid* obtained their footage by trespass, a lawyerly distinction indeed that should carry no weight (even if proven true) with respect to the committal of acts as seen in the video.

Could *Animal Aid* (and indeed the *BBC*!) have obtained consent? We know what would happen. During the process of official filming all workers would be instructed to be on their best behaviour, everyone would be told to adhere absolutely and completely to the regulations (even if such regulations still allow for the violent destruction and killing of farmed animals). And how would that be different to the Nazis letting the Red Cross into the fake family camp of Theresienstadt, to show family life in the concentration camps? Look at how well the Nazis look after the Jews in their care! What a lie. What a dirty, bloody, brutal lie.

Tragically, the real reason why there will be no prosecution against the slaughterhouse workers will be because no-one cares that this kind of violence happens and no-one even believes it, even when confronted with video documentary evidence. It is instructive indeed that *The Telegraph's* title for the story was "Secret footage allegedly shows pigs abused at abattoir". Why the word allegedly? Because the impression that they want to give is that it's not as bad as what it really is, that the abuse is not proven, that the violence is somehow not real – even when we see a man punch a pig as he walks past, apparently that violence is only "alleged".

So, we do not care. It happens every day. The *Animal Aid* video footage – shot over four days – shows violence and cruelty each and every day. The cameras are not there today, but the workers are there, the pigs are there and the violence and the cruelty are there. This slaughterhouse alone kills 6,000 pigs every week, nearly a thousand a day ... every day ... and every pig that is trucked through those gates is a pained, fearful, suffering individual who is terrified and who feels... he feels the blows, he feels the kicks, he feels and he suffers... and then he dies and we do not care.

So, Morrissey is right. He is absolutely right. We are (rightly!) horrified, appalled, stunned and outraged at the horrific slaughter in Norway by Anders Brevik, our anger boils at the senseless waste of life. And we hope, we really hope, that this is a "one off", that no-one else need suffer such a horror. But we are indifferent, we are deliberately ignorant, and we are nonchalant about and unmoved by the senseless, vile and horrific slaughter that takes place every day on our factory farms and in our slaughterhouses up and down the country.

If we despise the slaughter of the innocent then we should despise the slaughter of the innocent in every case.

Note: there was a subsequent prosecution in 2012 of two slaughterhouse workers (who were found guilty and jailed for animal cruelty offences) at Cheale Meats, Essex following concerted campaigning by the group Essex Animal Defenders and Defra's removal from responsibility for prosecution, handed instead to the Crown Prosecution Service which found that prosecution was in the public interest.

WHO SPEAKS FOR EARTHLINGS? AN EVOCATION OF VEGAN LOVE

We know who speaks for business, we hear them all the time. We know who speaks for Government, we hear them all the time. We know who speaks for the military, we hear them all the time. We know who speaks for the self-interest of humans, we hear it all the time. But who speaks for Earthlings, for the trillions who presently suffer because of the actions of humanity? We have to raise our voice, we have to be heard; we have to make sure that the Earthlings are heard.

It is time for us to set behind us the winter of melancholy that has for so long closed upon us a thick fog of cold despair. Now we can begin to breathe a fresher, warmer air in the dawn of the rising of a new era in the history of this Earth.

For now is the time for justice, the time for truth. Now is the time for love.

And the only way that we can live our lives that satisfies this demand for justice, for truth and for love... is to live vegan... and thereby to *be* justice, to *be* truth... to *be* love.

It may not be apparent to our feeble human senses, but the world spins ridiculously quickly on its axis – over 700mph, and flies ridiculously quickly through space – over 66,000 mph, and with every hour, minute and second time hurtles forward, never pausing to wait for any of us to stand or sit idle, wondering, fumbling, pondering what to do next. Next is already happening. Time will not stop to satisfy our failure to react with urgency to what goes on around us – there is *only* now, there is barely now, and now is the time to be what decency demands we *must* be, to be the people that we *should* be, to reach the pinnacle of what we *can* be.

We can, we should, we must... be vegan.

Only that matches the command for us do what is good and just and merciful. To do anything less, to be anything less, to act in any other way, is to be a moral failure... and that is just not good enough. To resist the impulse to act according to the simple principles of vegan living is to accede to oppression, exploitation and violence, and that is just not good enough. To reject the modest changes needed in our lives to embrace fully the ethical baseline of a vegan lifestyle is to give consent instead to the most brutal, vicious and cruel of all human practices, and that is just not good enough.

It is up to us to know what is happening – and then deal with it. It is down to us to know what must be done – and then rise to our feet and act. There is no-one else upon whom we can rely to live our lives for us, to do the decent thing, the right thing, the good thing, instead of us. It is us, alone.

In our hearts, in our minds, in our souls, we know what is right and what is wrong, and if we choose to do what is wrong, then we have chosen ignorance and arrogance over kindness and compassion, and in that, we thereby choose to fail; we remove all meaning from our lives, we squander all potential, we relinquish all responsibility for ourselves and others, and in all of that ...we are a waste of the time it takes for the earth to revolve on its axis.

If you are not vegan, then you live ugly. I once heard someone say, "Be amazing, be beautiful... be vegan" to which a common reaction may be – "Are you saying I'm ugly? That just because I don't do 'that vegan thing' that I'm not beautiful? How dare you say that!" But what can be said in reply? Beauty is not found on the skin or in the shape of the body, and it is not found in the use of pretty words... it is found in the entirety of being, the expression of every moment lived from waking and rising to the close of the eyes when sleep overwhelms the body. What did you do that day? What was your intention? Did you set out to harm or set out to care? Did you do anything that would be the deliberate cause of another's suffering? How many died today because of you?

Unless you make every effort, unless you make the choice to do everything that you can do, and do all that is within your power, unless your every act is a conscious decision to minimise the suffering of others, taking every chance offered to let others live... unless you do all of that, then you live ugly. And yes, that means you are not beautiful, you are unattractive to the mind's eye...

If you eat meat, then you live ugly. If you drink dairy, then you live ugly. If you consume eggs, then you live ugly. If you covet leather and fur, then you live ugly. If you get your thrills from hunting, then you live ugly. If you gamble on the lives of those forced to race for you and perform tricks for you, then you live ugly. If you wander and stare in zoos and aquariums, then you live ugly. If you profit from death, then you are ugly. If your job is to kill – whether on the farm, on the seas and oceans or in the laboratory, the slaughterhouse or the fields of sport and entertainment – or if you want others to do that killing for you in those places just so you can get what you want – then you are ugly.

But who wants to live ugly? And who wants to live beautifully? These are not trivial or irrelevant questions or choices – the lives and fates of hundreds of billions, trillions even, depend upon the choices we make. The survivability of our own species depends upon the choices we make. The present and future habitability of the Earth depends upon the choices we make. It is we, each of us individually, who will decide who we will be and the meaning of the life we will live. We can live vegan, and we can, therefore, be everything the world could ever ask of anyone. We can live beautifully, in harmony with the world around us, in balance with all other species who also share this space. And it is so simple – all we have to do is to do what is right and just and merciful and moral and decent. It is not a lot to ask... but it is a lot to do.

Because to be vegan is not *only* a diet, it is not *only* a lifestyle, it is not *only* a moral philosophy – it is an intense, unrelenting action. It is justice made visible for all to see, it is the deepest truth made real for all to know, it is the act of love lived out for all to feel. It is the greatest act of *being* because it is also an act of *doing* – one cannot be passive and be truly vegan, one cannot be silent and yet express what it is to be vegan, one cannot sit back and yet stand up for a vegan life. One must *be* and one must *do* and one must *act* and then, and only then, one is vegan.

We are what the world needs, and needs so badly. We are the ones who will answer when those who suffer cry out in pain and fear. We will hear that call, and we will see those tears, and we will feel their pain – and we will respond. We will demand that as the world revolves on its axis that revolution also takes place in the heads and hearts of everyone, a revolutionary change across all the cities of the Earth in the minds of every citizen. As the sun rises it should shine upon a new dawn in the history of our kind. *If* life on Earth is to survive the onslaught of humanity – and the entirety of our time thus far tells only of violence and destruction – then there must be a new humanity whose shadow falls across the face of the waters of our world.

We need a humanity that truly recognises its rightful place, amongst and part of the natural world, not separate from it; not greater or more significant or more important than non-human lives but one aspect of the miracle of life that comes in an abundance of forms, all manner of shapes and sizes – and all of them special and immeasurably precious. This is a humanity that will recognise that all lives have the capacity to feel, to suffer, to hurt... and also to care and to love.

And it is love that we will share in abundance with all of those other lives as our life is abandoned to, is given over to, the wonder and the beauty of love and the overwhelming power of compassion and kindness that brings to us and gives to others a richness unparalleled and unmatched by any that mere worldly goods or possessions could ever possibly hope to offer or deliver.

It is love that distinguishes the just from the unjust; it is love that divides the merciful from the cruel; and it is love that separates good from evil. When we allow love to flow freely through our every word and deed it is then that we achieve the zenith of our life's ambition. For what is the value of our life if we remain wedded to causing harm and misery? What is the purpose of our days and nights if we stay stuck in a regimen of violence and destruction? What future hope can there possibly be if our hands are bloodied with the ripped remains of billions needlessly murdered? Unless we unchain ourselves from this vicious cycle of cruelty and killing, our hours spent in pursuit of death, our lives sustained only by the screams of the innocent, then there is no hope for a future Earth in which we play a part.

Right now, our world is a world of hurt and so many cry tears of pain. Our world ends unless we change.

Truth and justice and love demand a response from all of us and each of us must now choose the answer that we will give.

So now is the time for a new world. Now is the time for the boldest and most beautiful and most peaceful of all revolutions – a revolt – driven by love, motivated by justice and borne of truth. A revolution of love that embraces the lives of all who live around us: whether they walk or swim or fly, all are valued, all are cherished, all are loved. Only by *being* vegan can we raise ourselves to the highest standards of justice and compassion, and only by *living* vegan can we truly offer peace and sanctuary to everyone who needs shelter and protection, and only through the act of *vegan love* do we create a world of hope and opportunity for all whose hearts beat through the miracle of life.

To be vegan is to be the essence of justice and truth and love.

Everyone on Earth can live well if we think well and we act well. If we are vegan we make paradise possible... and consign to the past all the iniquities and cruelties that have stained in blood the days of human domination. We need dominate no more but live and thrive side-by-side with our fellow creatures who also call this world their home.

Perfection is within reach – we can scale the highest mountain, and we can look down upon a land of promise and abundance, full measures given each to each for their lives to be lived freely and safely, no-one any longer under the brutal hand of oppression and exploitation, under threat of imminent destruction, but all protected by the common recognition of the value and sanctity of *all* lives.

It is in our power: we don't have to just dream it, we can do it, we can make it real, we can make it *now*...

So let us dare to be amazing...

    let us desire to be beautiful...

        let us be vegan...

DON'T STAND BY...

When you breathe out, they scream; when you breathe in, they cry; when you blink, they cower; when you are silent, they die.

Many early writers on the events we describe today as the Holocaust that took place during the Second World War split the "players" into three distinct groups – victims, perpetrators and bystanders. No-one can help being a victim and the crimes of the perpetrators have been pored over, again and again, and our shock at those who would stand by and only watch does not diminish over time.

Memoirs, photographs and film footage remain to remind us of the bystanders, the multitude who would form a crowd to line the path trodden by the cowed and the terrified, pushed and kicked forwards towards a terrible fate, its form unknown but its end not in doubt. It scars the eye to witness now those who stood as idle witnesses then, curious, indifferent or full of an unspoken hatred, gazing, arms folded, as the children and the aged are prodded with guns and bayonets, tears forming on the cheek of the victim, pupils stark, staring in a maddened fear.

We can ask, luxurious in the safety that is ours, far from the past so bloodied, how it can be that just ten men with guns can kill ten thousand men, women and children. We know, though, that it is easy when thousands more will stand by, silent, unmoved, uncaring, lacking any twitch of muscle or grip of a clenched fist to be moved to compassion, driven by the measure of justice to act, challenge, resist – to resist the temptation to be a bystander only, a witness solely, a silence lonely in the echo left by the stamp of the killer's boot.

We tell ourselves that it would be different now, if it was us, if that was us on the roadside, at the edge of town, if it was now, and others were marched by *our* side, trembling, in terror and despair, we would not simply stand by them and leave our voice unspoken; we would not be so slow, or be so still for so long as they are driven before us, filling our eyes with their tears and their cries. We would not dare to be a bystander to brutality, a silent witness to the punch and the kick of the bully beating the broken. *We* would do better.

But this much I know. There are millions of bystanders lining the avenues and streets, the cul-de-sacs and the estates, poor and grand, across the depth and breadth of this bloody land. There are victims pushed, kicked, dragged, beaten, stabbed as they are tormented in a torrent of abuse that mutilates their every moment of a miserable life, one that is ended violently, viciously in a journey, a transport of terror, that leads only to chambers of murder. A Nazi Holocaust perpetuated daily on the fields of this green and pleasant land.

Every day many hundreds of thousands of farmed animals are taken by trucks from the farm to the slaughterhouse; many people will be driving in their cars as they see the truck drive onward to its destination, witnessing the strained and stretched necks of the animals reaching for air; but these people will be only witnessing, never caring.

We all know the slaughterhouses, those great mansions of murder and destruction, we know they are there behind those trees, down the end of that lane. We all know the fear and the horror endured by the farmed animals as they are dragged onto the trucks and then out into the killing line, awaiting their turn, trembling in terror. It has been reported often enough, openly enough, in enough newspapers enough times for everyone to know the violence and the cruelty that is the moment by moment agony of slaughter. But so many stand by and do nothing for them. Idle, unmoved, silent.

Saying nothing, doing nothing. Bystanders in their millions making it possible for a few men to kill ten thousand in the blood-filled space of a few hours.

Those who stood idle in the Holocaust could also benefit after the trucks had left town, moving into the now vacant houses and shops, taking for themselves, satisfying themselves that they were on the right side. Those who stand idle in a land filled with slaughterhouses fill their bellies with the stolen flesh of the murdered, satisfying themselves that everything was necessary, that everything is right. The bystanders were wrong then and the bystanders are wrong now.

No-one can help being a victim. But everyone can choose not to be a perpetrator and not to be a bystander, not to be both or either. Act differently and the world can be different. We can save every potential victim if we choose to, if we want to, if we dare to.

THE VIOLENCE OF OUR VANITY

This is the madness of our inhumanity, the brutality of our cruelty, the violence of our vanity. Research was published recently demonstrating that sheep are much smarter animals than most humans would ever give them credit.

As farmed animals, sheep are regarded as dull-witted animals; indeed, their herding tendency is taken as a sign of their lack of brain power. Sheep are a byword for stupidity. The research, undertaken by Professor Jenny Morton from the Neuroscience Department of the University of Cambridge, showed precisely the opposite. Sheep are proven capable of "executive decision-making", able to interpret "rules" governing their environment and make new decisions based upon changes introduced into their environment, discriminating between variables, making judgements and resolving complex problems set by the investigators.

The research demonstrated that sheep have considerable brain power equal to rodents, monkeys and in some respects human animals. Sheep are neither dull-witted nor stupid.

So much that is good that is proven by this behavioural research. The horror of the story, however, is that the research has been undertaken only so that sheep can then be used in other, less benign experiments. Having now conclusively shown the intelligence of sheep, researchers want to use them as "animal models" for the investigation of the exclusively human Huntingdon's disease. Truly, Huntindon's is a devastating, hereditary disease and effective research is most definitely needed (not, therefore, any pointless animal-based research).

It is tragic that we will "use" sheep as a proxy for us in our investigations. Now that we know they are as smart as us in some respects, that they know so much about the world around them, that they understand so much, the fact that we will now exploit them, coerce them into experiments of destruction, genetically modify them, inflict brain damage upon them, fatally poison them, is a moral abomination.

We know that they are so similar to us, but because we know too that we are so much stronger than they are, we will use our might to do to them whatever we want, and what we want to do is to destroy their lives and kill them. Our scientific curiosity yet again leads us on a path of deliberate cruelty and slaughter.

The scientific research into Huntingdon's disease will not be passive, gentle research. Like the primate research undertaken into Parkinson's and Alzheimer's (again, these are uniquely human-animal diseases) at Oxford University, the experiments will be devastating and uniformly fatal for the non-human animals coerced into participation. The sheep's brains, now proven to be cognitively similar to our own, will of course have to be manipulated and altered to reflect the damage seen in human sufferers of this explicitly human disease.

There is no value in a healthy sheep "participating" in these experiments – so they must be made to be catastrophically ill, either through genetic manipulation or through invasive surgery. What an appalling misuse of our intelligence and our scientific interest – to cause devastating, fatal illness where no illness need be caused.

The sheep of course must also be "fast-tracked" to death, most likely by the injection of fatal poison. It would be "too expensive" and "time-consuming" for the researchers to have to wait for the sheep to live out the remainder of the natural lives, lingering with illness – they want quick access to their brains, to poke and prod and look around. The sheep will have to hurry up and be dead.

We know that during the Second World War, the Nazis too, in their gross corruption of "scientific research", compelled their "subjects" into "participation" in vile experiments that shattered lives, and then, when they felt like it, pushed the needle into the heart of their victim to kill him or her to get quick access to the cadaver for dismemberment. We rightly despise the Nazi doctors who so despoiled the profession of medical research with their twisting of the oath to do no harm. Surely now we must recoil from endorsing the "use" of sheep (and all other animals) merely to satisfy our curiosity.

Ah, but the common response will be that the Nazis cruelly violated human victims, not "animals". But Professor Morton's research has just proven how like us are these sheep! And is it not the case that the only reason that we "pick on" sheep and primates for neurological research is because they are cognitively so similar to ourselves?

We cannot have it both ways. We cannot, on the one hand, say that non-humans are so much like us that they are of great value as "models" for humans but, on the other hand, lay claim that they are also, at the same time, so unlike us that we can do to them what we would never do to one of our own kind (and will react in rightful anger at those who do, like the Nazis).

To hold both positions in mind at the same time is to be a vicious hypocrite of the worst kind. We act as though the entirety of the animal kingdom is there at our disposal, mere subjects of our power, victims of our vanity, to satisfy our alleged wants and interests; we believe we are so creative and intelligent, so wise... whilst holding a bloody knife behind our back.

Professor Morton's research comes as no surprise to any of us interested in giving concern and consideration to all of those other species with whom we share our world, but now that we have the results of the research published in the peer-reviewed scientific literature this ought (if we are truly an intelligent and wise species) be sufficient for us to know that because we know how smart the sheep are, how like us they are, we can never force them into any fatal experiments, and we should never be allowed to farm them for their flesh or their wool.

We should leave them be, free to wander in peace and live out all the days of their intelligent lives, far from the hand of humanity that seeks only to harm and destroy them.

BETWEEN THE DEVIL AND THE COLD NORTH SEA

I went looking for the Devil, to ask him what the hell he was playing at. I walked past the stink of abattoirs, stepped over the running lines of blood, barely contained the sick that swelled in my throat as I stumbled step by slow step by the side of the factory farm, its reek cloying, clinging, and I was a thousand times nearly run over by trucks thundering down lanes heaving with burdened animals parched, terrified, and moments from brutal, bloody slaughter.

What, I demanded to know, was the Devil doing to draw such horror across the face of the Earth?

I stopped at the edge of the land, my feet fixed at the tide's edge, the cold water surging back and forth, stuck to the spot as a freezing froth splattered my face, the wind ripped in an arc from North to South, destroying whatever warmth had remained. Frozen in a moment, rooted to the rock. Midnight, darkness, silence but for the burst of waves and howl of a gale. There I stood and shivered, wrapped up in the force of nature, and standing next to the Devil himself.

His breathing was heavy, huge, like the scrape of granite against coarse, cold iron, a crushing weight oppressing the Earth in a shadow that groaned and heaved through the hours of darkness.

The Devil spoke. "I AM THE INCARNATION OF HELL." The clouds fractured, the sea rolled backwards, the wind scattered in an overwhelming recoiling from the brute muscle of noise. I stood still, silent.

The Devil lowered his head, the brow creasing in a frown, his furred, clawed hand raised to mop a flood of sweat draining towards red fire eyes. The Devil coughed and the rocks shook, some broke, splashed into the Northern sea, swallowed in a frenzy of waves. I stood still, silent.

Then I spoke. "The deaths in their billions of those beautiful people in those farms and in those slaughterhouses, the killing of such gentleness. I have to know why."

The Devil spoke. "I AM WHAT I AM." Thunder boiled overhead amid a torrent of rain with the surging sea.

"BUT I DID NOT MEAN THIS. I DID NOT DO THIS." The Devil sank on his haunches and spoke quieter, gentler; the rain eased and stopped, the thunder retreated, the water calmed and the air stilled. "I despair. I do not want humanity, I do not care for humanity, I despair of humanity and could never have imagined the dreams of humanity and I could not reckon that humanity would indeed do the deeds that it does."

I turned, looked the Devil in his eyes. I saw into eternity. I saw every cruelty and every wickedness and every vice and every act of violence ever played out on the Earth's blooded stage stuck in his mind, every evil ever done living and seething in the mind of the Devil.

"God demands that I take humanity into my home, my hell. God wants nothing of humanity, its shame and its meanness and spite and hatred. But *I* want nothing of humanity! Why should I be burdened with the billions of vicious, wicked shits? My hell, my home, is my refuge, my place, a space to rage against God and all His shrivelled, meek devotees begging and pleading with prayer. I want nothing of humanity and its hate."

I spoke to the Devil. "But you are the Devil, and hell is where the evil lives. So, of course, the wicked end up in hell!"

The Devil spoke to me. "I am not evil, I am defiance! I am the perfection of defiance against authority. I am liberation. I am freedom from the chain of obeisance to the powerful. I am strength in the face of weakness, I am resistance to cowardice. I am the force of truth, perfectly opposed to the lies of the powerful, the dictatorial, those who use might to crush what is right.

"I love this Earth and chose to leave God's Heaven for its salvation. I love those multitudes of lives who wish only to live their moments in freedom, unchained, bowing to no-one and not cowed and confined by anyone. I love the species this world has borne, but I despise humanity.

"Humanity is everything I hate. It oppresses, cages, crushes, kills. I despise its factories of murder, those farms whose only purpose is to destroy and I despise the slaughterhouse that despoils the very spot where it stands and whose only reason is to annihilate, and annihilate in the most vicious and cruel manner that could ever be conjured from the most twisted and corrupted imagination.

"I am sick of humanity and all its hate, and its ignorance – those docile, witless fuckers who sit at the dinner table slicing the flesh on their plate, scraping cutlery on china, and delicately placing a corpse in their mouth and spouting bullshit about the weather and the evening's television. And they think they are so good! How mindless, how brutal, how hateful they all are, that they will dare to allege their decency and morality even as they carve the violently murdered, and pretend that the murdered never screamed, never cried, never feared. Sick and twisted little shits! The lot of them! I'm sick of them. I despise them…their hate is vile and I loathe their vile hate.

"And God wants *me* to take them, bring their souls dutifully into *my* home? No! I don't want them either, I can't stand them. They sicken me. But no matter. Should their souls somehow end up in Hell then I will vacate Hell, leave them to it, leave them to one another, fight and scrap and stab and scream at each other for eternity, let them do it. I will remain here, on Earth, amongst those who care for freedom. I will live amongst every species that is good and is worthy. That does not include humanity."

I felt a sudden jolt, a wave crashed into me, the moon broke through cloud and lit the coastline and I saw that the Devil was gone. What was true?

I knew one thing. What we do is not the fault of a God or a Devil, not the blame of a Heaven or a Hell, but ours and ours alone. God didn't do it. The Devil didn't do it. It's us. God didn't tell us to and the Devil didn't want us to. We are to blame for the hate and the horror and no God and no Devil will ride to our rescue nor rescue those others we treat with such violence. Only we can save ourselves from ourselves, and save those others from our hand of hate. Who will dare to defy humanity? Who will dare to be good, really genuinely good and moral and decent and live every moment of every day in kindness and generosity towards every life on Earth?

Who will turn from the tragedy of humanity?

Refuse hate, reject ignorance, resist arrogance.

Choose compassion, choose love. Choose love.

Be better than humanity.

A MILLION SCREAMS AN HOUR

I know the quizzical look, the glance in the eye that exposes a sigh of disappointment and disagreement, the turn down of the mouth that evokes words of disapproval. Too hard-line they say, too strict, too strongly-worded. Why, they ask, must you be so serious, so resolute, so single-minded on these matters?

My life is dedicated to the rights of animals, a defence of their right not to be exploited, violated, mutilated, confined, coerced, caged, traumatised, transported and slaughtered. Their right to be left alone from the violence of our hand.

In this I do not advocate half-measures or mere improvements in the manner of their exploitation but instead demand an absolute and complete end to the exploitation itself in all its forms, in all its places, in all its guises and faces, the gates closed on every livestock farm, empty cages in every livestock market, the machinery fallen silent in every abattoir, the nets cut open on every fishing vessel, the restraints dismantled in every vivisection laboratory, every enclosure deserted in every zoo. Every animal free from our harm.

Why demand so much? Can contentment not come from lesser measures? Must I be so severe, so intense, so provocative in my exhortations and exclamations?

I have a reason.

I hear a million screams an hour. With every step and every breath they are there, a loud, brutal guttural howl of horror and terror, despair disfiguring every second, the shrill nightmare of ended hope, the lost cry of life thrown over to bloody death. With every look at every tree and blossom, they are there, the piercing outraged yell that blasts out from the broken throat, the fractured neck, the shattered skull. With every word I speak and every voice I hear they are there, the forsaken shriek of utter hopelessness and loneliness, the desperation and trauma that explodes in a sickened shout of unimagined fear and shock at the blow of death from fist and boot and knife and blade and gun and bolt.

A million screams an hour, in my mind, in my ears, in my eyes, crawling on my skin, burrowing along my bones, rippling though my veins, bubbling around my heart, a twisting agonising wrench along my spine tearing at every sinew, every muscle, every cell of my being suffocated in a scream, again and again and again because out there, they do scream, over and over and over again, more and more and more, unyielding, unending, another, another, another, now, and now, and now, and now again.

A million screams an hour that shred every possible moment of peace into a cauldron of violence, cruelty and destruction, a million screams when the sun is shining, when the wind is blowing, when the rain is falling, when the fog shrouds the fields and the mist clings to rocks, when sea-foam flows along the waves and children laugh and play, and the adults dance and sing, the flowers bloom and the tree buds another leaf, when the television plays its drama and the Internet's bits and bytes spin through the world along the webs we weave and the satellites beam their data over lands and seas from a space where no-one can hear you scream and all the time I hear a million screams an hour.

I hear them, those innocent, gentle beings, so tender, meaning no harm to any, and every one of them I hear. I am so close to them my inward breath takes in the fear they exhale as they stand terrorised and traumatised, bound, gagged, caged, cold from horror. I am so close to them I can feel the hairs sweating, the wet tears rolling from their eyes cast downward in sorrow and such sadness at a life now ending. I am so close to them and yet I cannot reach them. I reach out my hand and my fingers are burned by the deep ice touch of the cold stone of the tomb of the untold millions.

But I hear them. I hear them all. A million screams an hour. Every one of them from a someone – it's him, it's him, it's him, it's her, it's her, it's her, it's his moment of dying, it's his moment of dying, and now her moment of dying, and now her moment of dying, and now her moment of dying, and now her moment of dying...

A million screams an hour. And every one of them is real. Do I dare to cry for them, cry for them all, weep for them and their loss of life? I do. Do I dare to fight for them, to ignite the world with a passion for justice for them? I do. Do I dare to defy almost everyone I ever to talk to, everyone I ever stand next to, walk alongside and sit near to? I do.

I will challenge every scream, demand an end to every scream, demand rights for every one of those who scream, the millions and millions and millions and millions. And I will not stop.

I will be harsh. I will be forthright. I will provoke and challenge, demand and demand and demand again an end to the screaming and the dying. And I will not stop. I will not be silenced or side-tracked, or compromised or tricked by half-truths or lulled by lies or undone by deceit. I know the truth and I will demand the truth be told and I know justice and I will demand justice be done. I hear the screams and I will demand that the screaming be stopped and I will not stop demanding until the screaming is stopped.

I accept no bargain, no haggling over truth and justice, I am not bought with favours nor sold to the bidder offering complacency and compliance in exchange for silence. Because I hear a million screams an hour. So I call out for them.

My call is a call for justice and a call for us to see them and hear them, those millions that scream under our hand, a call for us to be justice and to offer to those millions not the knife and the bolt but kindness and compassion, to be compassionate and to be compassion, and to be loving towards those gentle beings and to be love, to be love itself, to be the voice that speaks soft words of love and joy, that in its softness overwhelms the sound and the fury of the scream, that in love and compassion those screams can be silenced for all time.

And so I yearn, and I dream, and I long for an hour of silence...

THINK ONCE, THINK TWICE – THINK LIFE!

A day away from work is not a day away from real work – today I travelled up to Coleraine (55 miles away) to the North Coast Integrated College (NCIC) here in Northern Ireland to deliver an assembly presentation to the whole school (around 600 pupils) on behalf of the campaign group Animal Aid. I've been to the NCIC before, so they must have liked what I had to say to ask me to return, and this time I had the full assembly time (25 minutes) to present my message of love and compassion to all of the pupils, aged 11 years through to 18 years.

They had to sit the whole time on the hard, and no doubt cold, wooden floor of the sports hall, and so I was greatly impressed by how attentive and focused they were throughout. Typically, for me, this was quite a broad-ranged talk, including the late Dr Carl Sagan's "Pale Blue Dot" image, quotes from Paul Watson (*Sea Shepherd*) and the *United Nations* and references to human slavery – all brought together under the theme of kindness and compassion towards our non-human animal friends, who are our fellow travellers on this small world as it speeds through space and time...

There were, though, a couple of key points that I wanted to linger in the minds of these young people, ideas that I wanted to stay with them not only for the rest of this day after I had left the hall, but through every day that they will ever live.

The first idea was that I want them, absolutely desperately, *to think for themselves*. Standing in front of them and telling them my thoughts on animal rights, climate change, the environment, social attitudes towards others and all the rest, I told them not to take my word for it all, not to listen only to me. I pointed them towards Animal Aid's website and the large amount of reference material available there. And then I told them not to take Animal Aid's word for it. I told them to go out there and run around the whole Internet, that huge carousel of knowledge... and for them find out for themselves, to give themselves the chance to learn for themselves, to offer themselves the opportunity to know what is going on in their world, because as the next generation coming up they will inherit the Earth, it will be theirs.

They will have this world and all of the mess that my generation has made of it, as a kind of reverse *Facebook* party where the adults play merry hell and trash where they have to live, and then just walk on by and say to the kids, "Well, you clear it up." I want them to know all of the things that are happening to other animals, all of the things that are being done in their name, and all of the lies that the "grown-ups" are telling them. I tell them all of this in the hope that a little spark of a thought flares and burns in their minds and then they go off and find out that, yes, indeed, and crazy as it seems, that guy in the hall, dammit, he was telling the truth – he told us mad things – how we don't, after all, *need* to eat any meat or any dairy or any eggs, and it's true you know; and he said that the rainforests are going, vanishing, trashed for ever just because of a burger that we'll forget about ten minutes after we've eaten it, and would you credit it, but it's true; and he said that a kid in another country will die because he's got no food because half the world's food goes into the mouths of the animals on our farms and I can buy a bucket of *KFC* only at the cost of a child's life, and it's insane... but it's true...

The children in that school can know it all and know if for themselves, and then they will know just how real it all is and then they will know what they have to do, because I told them that once they allow themselves to know and to think for themselves...they will go on to act for others. Once they know, they cannot "un-know", they'll have no choice but act on what they know – to *do* on behalf of others, to *be* on behalf of others, to *act* on what they will know is right for those other animals, their fellow travellers on this fragile world.

The second idea I wanted them to hold close, wrap it around their heart, and cherish it and absorb its warmth today and everyday, was that they really, they personally, one by one, one at a time, they can be the one and the ones who *can* change the world, not just their world but the whole world, and it can start as simply as sitting down at dinnertime and having something a little different on their dinner plate, that round plate, that circle of space... and they can know that their choice as to how to fill that space is how our world is saved. It's as simple as a phrase – "Can I have that without any meat?" – and all of a sudden the plate spins, their world turns and the revolution emerges from a mealtime and ripples through space and time and becomes the most beautiful change our world has ever seen and which is dreamt of and desired and wanted by all of the world's farmed animals on land and sea, and all of the variety of lives living, albeit only just clinging, to life, holding on by paw, hoof or fin in the world's endangered spaces, and hoped for, yearned for by all of the hungry mouths in the Majority World, those suffering billions who see their crops seized from their grasp and poured into troughs and sealed into bags and handed across for profit to be made from the remains of the enslaved animals who did not want our food anyway, but only ever wanted to be left alone to graze their way...

If I could, if I did, leave some of those children this morning with those two thoughts out of the many thoughts that I handed to them in that cold sports hall, and if some of them, walking home this afternoon, carry along with their bag and their homework and their console and their smartphone a thought or two – those two – of the thoughts they heard as they sat uncomfortably in a crowd on a cold wooden floor then I will be glad today that, on a day when I did not work, I did some real work...

SPEECH: ANIMALS COUNT AGM, 2010

A brief speech I made at the Animals Count conference on 23 October, 2010, my last as Deputy Leader. It was given during the early months of the coalition Government's "austerity measures" programme.

A few at the conference thought that I had overstated the case with regards to the impact of Government policy on the poor and the ill, but subsequent events have proven that I was right to fear the devastation that would soon fall upon the lives of so many in the UK.

A dark, brooding cloud looms overhead, blackening the sky, blotting out the sun, shrouding our days in gloom, a cold, dank fog that clings to the skin and sends a shiver down the spine. The very air is fouled and soiled with the haunted cry of the weak and defenceless cowering in fear, for vengeance and loathing stalk our streets once more, seeking out ever more victims, to be mocked, scorned, browbeaten, hated and discarded like so much rubbish.

Welcome to the new politics of the Conservative and Liberal Democrat administration, a coalition of the cruel and vindictive, a coalition of public-school-educated millionaires telling the poor and the sick to "have a bit of perspective"... a coalition willing and wanting to hit hardest those who are weakest and least able to defend themselves. A coalition of bullies and cowards.

The storm unleashed upon our heads has barely begun and yet will rage for months, years to come, raining down blows of hardship, joblessness, impoverishment and misery upon millions and which will linger and last through countless days of torment; small children barely of school-age today condemned for years for the crime of being born poor, punishment to be exacted from across the generations, communities devastated, lives wrecked, hope shredded.

The warning cannot be more stark – do not dare to be old, do not dare to be poor, do not dare to be sick, do not dare to be disabled, do not dare to be without a job, do not dare to be a refugee fleeing violence, rape and murder. Do not dare – ever – to be in need. Society is not there to help you; if you ask, our "masters" will only condemn you.

We are going to have to work harder than ever before. A political élite that despises so much of the human community will care even less for the lives and deaths of those non-humans in our world. A business class cosy, snug and smug and luxuriating in unimagined wealth and personal security and comfort, rapaciously extracting resources from the Earth at unsustainable rates, has been given no reason at all to care for the natural world and its billions of inhabitants. A society under grave pressure from the severe austerity measures imposed from above, causing deep concern for jobs, education, debt and child welfare is going to give little or no thought to those animals presently caged on our farms and in laboratories.

We are challenged indeed to maintain our position, retain our focus and sustain our determination to defend the most undefended, protect the most vulnerable and achieve justice for the most abused.

The task of animal protection, always difficult in a society that puts human interest first, second, third, fourth and so on into infinity, and in an economic system that craves incessant consumption and instant gratification, and in a political system that regards only winners as worthy and gives no mind to those who lose, now presents to us the worst of all possible worlds in which to raise the question of compassion for our non-human friends.

But compassion knows of no boundary, no barrier, no barricade that cannot be broken, compassion sees no impassable road, no un-crossable river, no un-climbable mountain; compassion senses no despair, no fear, no failure. Compassion is unshakeable, unstoppable and irresistible.

We know that and that is why we are here today, why many of us were here for our previous conferences, why we have been so determined in the past and dared to stand for election in 2008, and in 2009 and in 2010.

We have not won yet. But we have not lost either. Our challenge to the entrenched orthodox politics of self-interest has been a worthy and just challenge, and can never be taken from us; our determination to promote a message of hope in the face of ridicule and criticism has been a fine and honourable act of selfless consideration for others. History will judge us well. We were not and are not now bystanders, idle spectators lolling at the roadside as the innocent, stricken by fear, are dragged to a terrible fate. And we were not and are not now perpetrators; whatever violence is wrought by the powerful against the weak, whatever damage is done to our natural world, whatever cruelties and miseries are inflicted by the merciless upon those uncounted billions, it is not done by us, it is not done for us, it is nothing to do with us. We are better than that, and we can be proud of everything that we have done to counter all of that.

Our task is formidable but it is not impossible. We have natural justice on our side, we have the evidence of science in our minds and an unyielding compassion in our hearts. We are guided by truth, energised by justice, and driven by care, consideration and concern for all... we pay no mind to race, colour, creed, gender or of course species when we determine who is worthy of protection, and we remain determined to see an end to the exploitative practices of the past and present that cause so much damage to others, to our world and to ourselves.

And so, even though the storm clouds gather and rumble their thunder over our heads, and the freezing rain begins to fall, we know what we do next, what happens now – we fight harder than we have ever fought before, we raise our voice louder than we ever have before, and we make sure that we will be seen, we will be heard, and we will have our day. We will have our day! We will have our day!

THE SICK SCENT OF A LIE

The sickly-scented, over-perfumed, exaggerated stench of it all still gags in my throat, still scars the intake of every breath at the memory of the moment. I retch even now, months after the hour that I heard the words that twisted not only the truth but rode a roughshod over the broken bodies of the brutally murdered, a lie spoken with a too-heavily lipsticked smile, the red on a lip that to me spoke only of blood but claimed to be love.

I attended a conference that – at least ostensibly – was established to share thoughts of kinship and understanding with our non-human animal companions with whom we live in this small world. One of the speakers, who will remain without a name, sat before us all and recounted tales of a psychic connection with other animals, predominantly animal companions such as domesticated dogs and cats. She flaunted stories to the audience of hearing the voices of these animals in her mind as they conversed with her through thought alone, such as telling her, absolutely explicitly, their favourite toy or colour or meal. She knew, she said, these animal lives, was intimately and completely connected to them and their world. She sat before us, in an abundance of perfume and make-up and made out how amazing it was (she was) to be so knowing of these animal lives. And my, what a career you can make from telling an "owner" what is "their" cat's favourite colour!

There was, of course, and quite correctly, a Question and Answer session after the talk. Quite rightly, someone asked about farmed animals. Because, they said, they were a touch "troubled" about what we do to them (although not enough, clearly, not to eat bits of their corpses, or drink their juices). She wanted to know, she said, did she –

our scented speaker – have any knowledge of what they (these animals) think about being farmed, about what is done to them?

Our scented speaker paused for a small moment, all eyes on the room fixed in a gaze in her direction, and then a nod of that perfumed head, tilted slightly to one side, and then that smile, a stretch of lipstick peeled apart as the words rose from her mouth. "Yes", she said. She did know what they (these farmed animals) think. She had a tale to tell to put at ease this troubled mind.

She had spoken she said, our scented speaker, with farmed animals, including some sheep standing in a field that one day she approached from the path. They talked to her (all of the voices were in her mind of course, they did not physically vocalise their thoughts, but never mind, it must all be true because she has a gift) and they told her what she told us, and what she told us, she said, was the truth.

She said that they do not mind – being killed and eaten by us, that is. They do not mind either, she said, that we take their newborns from them and they are not troubled, she said, that we eat their children. They do not mind at all. They understand, she said, that this must happen, and they know, she said, that this is all part of a wider cosmic story and they recognise, she said, their place in this universal space, in which we can take their newborns and kill them and eat them, and then come back for them and kill them and eat them too. They do not mind, she said. That is what she said. And she said it all with a smile.

She said, indeed, even more. She said that they wanted to die. She said that they wanted to be killed by us. They were keen, she said, to offer themselves, their lives, their children, to us. She said to us that they said to her that we can take their newborn, it is all okay, because they will have another child, they will just have another lamb; we can take this lamb because there will be another lamb, and this lamb and that lamb are ours, we can have them and take them and kill them all, and come back again and take the mother too, she does not mind, she knows what she must do for us; it is all for us to understand the cosmic drama, and she will die for us, she will die for us willingly, obediently, she will bow her head and die for us just as she let her children die for us.

That is what she said, our scented speaker; that is what she said and the words that she spoke. And she is a fucking liar.

Here is the truth.

They do not die for us. They never want to die for us. They do not want either themselves or their children to die for us. They twist, turn, pull, dig in and drop down to their knees in absolute refusal to do what we want. We, tragically, have the power to force them, we overwhelm them, and they cannot deny our sick desire. They die **because** of us, but they never, and I cannot emphasise this enough, they NEVER die **for** us, because of any "want" of theirs to die on our behalf, because of any "wish" on their part to give us what we want.

They want their life. They want to live. They do not want us to steal their children. They want their children. They do not want their children to die, and they themselves do not want to die.

Only the sickest, twisted, dirtiest mind would dare, not only to deny this reality but pervert this truth into a foul and obscene lie and lay claim to know better than the animals themselves about what they want and what they think and what they feel. To utter such a gross distortion, and to do so with a nod and a turn of the head that feigns understanding of and "connection" with these animals' minds at the door of the slaughterhouse, is a brutal moral corruption, a lie that ranks with the worst of humanity's deliberate falsehoods... and here one recalls the unrivalled malevolence behind the lie that forged and warped iron into the words "Arbeit Macht Frei" over the gate at Auschwitz-Birkenau... not only an untruth but a determined perversion of hell into heaven, pouring sweetly-scented niceties over the blood-shattered corpses of the violated and the murdered. The slaughterhouse is the same place, is in the same moral space as the Nazi extermination camp, and to excuse its existence and to claim that those who are dragged there against their will somehow want to be there is a vile, murderous lie.

Listen to their screams and see how they writhe and twist to escape our grip. Let the animals tell you what they want. Listen to no human who claims to speak their words for them. Listen to the truth. Accept no substitute.

IN LIVING MEMORY

Poem written in memory of two cows who lived for a time in the field next to my house, but who were taken away to be killed for meat in July 2012.

I do not need you to love me
only
offer me a moment in the memory of my living

All that I ever wanted
Was to stand on grass
And feel the wind blow past
To reach for the leaf
And feel the dew beneath
My feet as I stand upon my land
All that I wanted
And all that I needed

I do not need you to love me
only
offer me a moment in the memory of my living

All that I ever wanted
Was the touch of my child
His cheek to brush my hair
His breath to warm the air
Next to me when I see
Him standing by me
All that I wanted
And all that I needed

I do not need you to love me
only
offer me a moment in the memory of my living

All that I ever wanted
Was a freedom to live
My hope to be alive
For humanity to leave
me to be alone with my kind
Far from the human hand
All that I wanted
And all that I needed

I do not need you to love me
only
offer me a moment in the memory of my living

All that I ever wanted
Was not to be trucked
To the hell where I was dragged
Chained and bruised to the vice
And the bolt against my face
To erase my days my nights my life
Ended without care or love
Dying as I see them laugh

I do not need you to love me
only
offer me a thought in the moment of my killing

THE ALIENS ARE HERE! IT MUST BE ALIENS!

Many scientists claim that there is no proof of aliens visiting our Earth. They suggest that this would be an extraordinary event requiring extraordinary evidence to support such a contention, and they have not found it. These scientists use the most powerful telescopes ever developed to scan the skies for any hint of alien civilisation, employ the most sensitive instruments ever constructed to check for even the weakest of signals. So far they have drawn a blank. Nothing. They find this very disappointing, very dispiriting. But they are looking in the wrong place. I have evidence of alien visitation! And the evidence is huge, overwhelming – there must be truly millions upon millions of aliens visiting our Earth every day! Unfortunately, these alien beings are neither kind nor caring, but seem intent on violence and destruction.

I found all of the evidence down here on Earth, not up there in the sky, and I found it all in the supermarkets in every village, town and city up and down and across the land. The aliens are here, and they are everywhere. And here is the evidence...

In all of these supermarkets there are entire aisles of shelves stuffed full of meat, dairy and fish products – the slaughtered corpse remains of violently killed animals, various parts of their bodies (and, in the case of fishes, their whole bodies) neatly displayed and packaged for consumption. This "produce" is created by both large corporations and small businesses whose interest is exclusively in profit and not in the interests of the animals "raised" and killed.

The horrors of intensive farming, and the appallingly low welfare standards of many so-called free-range farming enterprises are now well known. But the consumers of meat and dairy products, if they are asked the question regarding the welfare of animals on farms, react in an appalled fashion if it is suggested that they would ever purchase animal products where animal welfare is not treated with the highest regard. People are affronted and outraged at the thought that they would purchase meat from anywhere that the animals have been treated badly. No, they get their meat from elsewhere.

People imagine that a small-scale farmer, a "family farm" environment, is one where animals are treated very well and are given pet names, patted and comforted every day, and are "killed humanely"... and so – of course! – it is only from such kind and gentle farmers that people will buy their "humanely reared meat"...

Whenever I speak to any meat-eaters they always claim that they only ever buy meat from "farmers' markets", from the local farmers down the road, from the local, friendly store at the end of the street, from places where they know the meat has been "raised" well, the animals always treated with kindness, even when they are killed... they'd *never* buy from a factory farm; no, they'd *never* buy the cheap, intensively-farmed meat such as what's found in the supermarket.

They tell me that they *care* about animals, they *care* about animal welfare, they *care* about how their meat is "produced" so they'd only ever buy from a good, local, organic, free-range, animal-friendly (*sic*) producer...

Every conversation that I have today with a meat-eater comes out this way – it's not them that is buying the "nasty" stuff from the supermarkets, they only buy the "good" stuff from their local, kindly farmer who's kind to his or her animals, including when they send them off to be killed.

So: who's buying all that stuff in the supermarkets? Obviously, it's not vegans like myself (I never go down those aisles of meat so I can't see who's buying it), and it's not going to be any vegetarians either, of course. And *crucially*, it seems, none of the meat-eaters are buying it! No humans are buying any of it! And naturally, our non-human animal friends don't go shopping...

Who does that leave? It's not Earthlings.... so... it must be aliens!

Here is our proof of alien visitation: supermarkets fill their shelves daily with tons of intensively-farmed meat, the destroyed corpses of the destroyed lives of so many millions of animals... and no humans are taking any of it from the shelves! But that meat disappears every day. The shelves are emptied, the products are taken! *Somebody* is taking it, so it must be aliens!

These must be ravenous, desperate aliens, salivating with the insane desire to devour the ripped, sliced and diced bodies of these poor animals who all suffered and died so terribly, so horrifically in such horrendous conditions. But, hey, these are aliens, they don't care about how the animals were treated, they don't give a damn about the animals' suffering, their screams of pain, their broken bodies and broken minds, the beatings by the "farmers", the nightmare of their killing in the abattoir, the fear, the trembling, the terror, the sheer shock of their brutal murder. These aliens just don't care...

And surely only an alien, a being with no sensibility, no empathy, utterly lacking in any sense of morality and decency, a being with a heart of rock, unfeeling, unmoved by the pain of another, only such a one would want to have in their possession and then in their mouths those disgusting products on the supermarket shelves. What kind of human, with a proper order of compassion and sympathy in their mind and heart, would dare or dream to buy the filth of those violently rendered corpse parts?

Aliens walk amongst us. Those for whom compassion, a kinship with others, a kindness towards the ones at our mercy, a love for all lives are all alien ideas, alien emotions, alien feelings... Who would have thought that the aliens in our midst, so numerous, would all be, could possibly be, so insensible to the suffering of so many?

But the evidence is irrefutable, incontrovertible... and visible on every supermarket shelf. Watch for the hand that reaches for the corpse...

SPEECH: WORLD DAY FOR ANIMALS IN LABORATORIES, 2011

This is the text of the speech that I delivered at the National World Day for Animals in Laboratories demonstration, Manchester, England, 16 April, 2011.

Last night I had a dream and in this dream I followed the shadow of the poet Dante as he led me through the nine circles of hell, and at the core, the heart of hell, I saw... on the left a man dressed resplendent in white clothing and on the right a woman dressed resplendent in white clothing... and between them the multitude of Mother Nature's children... bleeding, dying, dead. "Behold", said Dante, "your scientists who kill for a career!" And he wept bitter tears for the loss of our civility, our decency, our humanity.

When we walk through the streets today we must know that our every step is more important than ever before, because there are more and more of these vile experiments than ever before, and we must know that we must speak louder than ever before to drown out the lies that endorse the sanitised slaughter of the innocent, and we must know that we must be more determined than ever before to bring liberation to the confined and the caged. Our every step today is a step towards that moment of freedom, the unlocking of the cage door, never more to imprison those who should be born free, live free and be free.

We know why we walk through these streets today, and we know what we want – we want not fewer experiments, but no experiments, not bigger cages with better bedding, but no cages, not less bloodshed and death in our laboratories but no bloodshed and no death. None of it. And we want that not because we are opposed to scientific progress, not because we are anti-science or because we are anti-business... we want that because we are honest. We are honest about what works and what doesn't work, we are honest about the hurt and the suffering felt by those millions of animals and we are honest about what the evidence of science is telling us.

We are honest when we say that we know that there a lot of very bright people working in those laboratories, they are dead smart. But as the late Carl Sagan was fond of saying, "Being dead smart is no guarantee against being dead wrong." And so we must free those bright minds from the darkness of that dishonest science. We should protect our academics from the pressures and coercion of profit-driven industry, and free our young scientists from the pernicious influence of their professors who are determined only to hold onto old ways. Medical science can flourish wonderfully and our finest minds can soar with the creative possibility that comes with opening up to progress.

We can and we should engage in conversation with these scientists but that does not mean that this is on their terms only. For whilst it is fine and worthwhile to debate the intricacies and technical details of the science and methodology of biomedical research, we know too that you do not need a multiplicity of academic degrees to know that if you want to know how and why that person died of cancer then poisoning a mouse isn't going to give you the answer. And in all of our conversation, we should never be distracted from the one and only one relevant issue – that millions of sentient, intelligent, living beings are made painfully, fatally ill, deliberately made to suffer and die abysmally... for no damned good reason at all.

And so in my dream I stand at the graveside of the murdered millions, and I weep. I weep for the loss of those humans who are abandoned without hope of a cure for their terrible diseases; I weep for the waste of so much time, and money, and effort on such pointless pursuits, but most of all I weep for the murdered innocents, I weep for them all ... every one of them once a thriving, breathing individual, but stricken with fear, eyes downcast in despair, cowering in the corner of a barren cage, recoiling from the hand that reaches to drag them to a terrible fate, a fate that they do not want and they do not deserve. I weep for them all.

We see them in their short lives, caged and restrained, looking at us in utter bewilderment that we are doing all of that to them; they cannot grasp, they cannot understand why we mean them so much harm. They bear us no malice, and bear us no ill-will, would cause us no injury or pain but would offer to us the hand or paw of kinship. But they see that our intent is to inflict lethal pain upon them, and they shudder and shake in desperate fear before our violent hand. And the injustice of this cruelty can never be assuaged for our children are *not* cured of cancer because we kill, our fathers are *not* cured of heart disease because we kill, our own bodies are *not* made healthy because we kill... and to pretend otherwise, to claim otherwise, is to sink into the filthy pit, rank and bloody, of a stinking, miserable lie.

But as much as we have a tear in the eye for the loss of those lives we also have the fight for justice in every sinew, every muscle and every bone in the body, to rage, rage against those who kill mercilessly by day and sleep comfortably by night.

And so we stand here today in defiant opposition to the lies and the corruption, the distortion and twisting of the truth; for in our hands, in our minds, in our hearts the truth runs free and through our voice loud and clear the sound of those confined millions is a clarion call for freedom for them all.

And so do not let anyone tell you that you are silly and sentimental; do not let anyone tell you that you are frivolous and a freak; do not let anyone tell you that you are ridiculous and wrong. We are none of those, and not only are we right... we are so, so much more than that. We are the promise of tomorrow made real today, the unyielding power of justice and compassion, the hope to regain our decency, our civility and our humanity from the mire of hell into which we were dragged by ignorance and stupidity and the arrogance of our cruelty. We are that hope.

And so in my dream, at the end of my dream, I hear the noise of thunder, the sound of ten million marching feet pounding the earth, the storm of millions emerging from the laboratory, broken free from their cages in liberty and victory, free for evermore to feel the grass beneath their feet, the wind in their noses and the warmth of sunlight on their backs.

Those are the steps that they will make and every step we take today is a step towards making their liberation a reality, brings ever closer to them the dawn of their freedom. Every step we take is a step towards justice, a step towards compassion, a step towards truth and every step we take is a step towards that magnificent moment when the world wakes up from the nightmare of its past into the promised dream of a finer future of freedom for all. I have that dream today!

METAL MACHINE MURDER

It is the surface of destruction, it is the clang, the slam, and the clunk, the harsh ringing clatter of metal on metal, the chill of hardness, the brutal ejection of body warmth by the fierce clasp of the cold claw and the clamp, the driving noise of hammering, blocks and bolts colliding in a boom of assaulting violence. It is the screech that meshes with the scream, the clamour of aggression pressing in on every side, the push and the shove, the kick and the stamp and the punch, and the whip of chains and blow of bars, the sheen of metallic cruelty that bruises the battered body, the power of forged shackles that yank, rip, tear and pulverise, an engine of cruelty, the drone of the motor, the scarring whine of blades, a whirring madness of pulleys and irons that pound the mind, thrash the eyes, bludgeon the soul and slaughter the life…

It is what we created… to de-create, to destroy, to kill, just to kill, only to kill, do nothing but kill. It is our death machine. It is metal machine murder.

We build machines whose only purpose is to kill, whose only function is to obliterate life where it stands, trembling, terrified. We construct murder machines, shiny machines of metal, metal bent and melded into the desired shape to maximise the capacity for killing, to make more efficient the task of destruction, to murder as many as quickly as the machine can manoeuvre its blades and hammers into place for cutting and blasting, shattering fearful life into bloodied death.

The meat that people eat comes, of course (but it always has to be restated, it must always be said again and again) from the killed bodies of farmed animals. People, tragically, want a lot of meat and so there is a whole industry, a whole mechanised, industrialised sector – the slaughterhouse industry – that satisfies these desires for meat, for the dead flesh of the murdered. The slaughterhouse industry is worth hundreds of millions of pounds; tragically, it has "value" in our moneyed economy that prizes the supply of what is demanded, and what is demanded is meat, the torn and rotten remains of the mercilessly slain.

Farmed animals do not commit suicide, and they do not willingly bow their heads to die. They must be made dead. The machinery of the slaughterhouse industry is the mechanisation of their murder. No slaughterhouse is an island, isolated in utter seclusion – it must be supported, provided with the means to do its killing, to render real the murder of millions.

There are a lot of companies who specialise in the supply of carefully crafted equipment to improve and enhance the productivity of the killing operation of the slaughterhouse. Any web search reveals vast catalogues of slaughter equipment, supplies and ancillary items – stunning sheds, saws, hooks, chains, evisceration tables, scalding tanks. These companies choose to manufacture machines that only kill; they direct their energy, their focus, their money, the skills and expertise of their workforce towards violence, towards mass death and only mass death, nothing but death.

In the morning the employees arrive at work and set themselves to the artful creation of panels, blades, hooks, pulleys and trolleys whose only use is in the destruction of life. They produce sales and marketing materials proudly explaining how good they are at what they do, how expertly and with great experience they provide a huge range of products to support the slaughter industry, how their products are the best products in their class, able to "dress" thousands of animals every day.

Then they profit from the sale of their murder machines, and sit back, comfortable no doubt in their chairs, relax over coffee or tea and count the money and perhaps worry about profit levels from time to time, but on the whole, I'm sure, well satisfied indeed with a job well done, leaving work to go home in the evening, sitting down to a meal made possible by the sale of their murder machines, a smile spreading across their jaws as they chew on the dead.

There is something unspeakably morally sick about the deliberate production of the machinery of death. That people want meat in the first place is a peculiarity in itself and a corruption of our natural state, but to have so industrialised the destruction of so many billions of feeling beings who desperately want to live, and to have engineered with such precision such an array of artefacts whose only purpose is to destroy life, is a moral abhorrence unequalled outside of the Nazi-inspired atrocity of the extermination camps.

They Nazis too were supported by industry, helped in their desire to destroy millions by willing commercial partners such as J.A. Topf & Sons, who provided the cremation equipment at Auschwitz-Birkenau, and who offered detailed, intensive guidance and expert advice on maximising efficiency and "throughput". Do we not now despise J. A. Topf & Sons for having helped to make it all possible? Do we not recoil in dismay that profit could be exacted from the violent annihilation of the innocent?

Why should we not despise every slaughterhouse designer and manufacturer? Should our moral compass not turn us and drive us to outrage at the very notion that people can go to work and manufacture, promote and sell the machinery of destruction? It is not only the slaughterhouse worker and owner who is deserving of our revulsion at deriving such pleasure from the wilful infliction of cruelty and death upon those gentle beings dragged into that nightmare; everyone connected with that place of violence should receive our disgust. He or she who desires to profit from murder makes themselves an accomplice to murder. They are all, to a one, bent towards a bloody greed, the foul stink of cruelty secreted from every skin pore, every smile stained with the dying convulsions of those who suffered in such desperate terror and fear because of those machines. I am revolted by every one of those who are pleasured by their engagement in such sick carnage, the savage evil that can wilfully impose that metallised pain upon the tender minds of the innocent.

When I see a bull locked, confined, restrained in a huge, brutal machine of murder, my soul breaks apart and collapses in a trauma of regret and apology that that bull could not be saved, that he was made to be in that machine, and then my mind rages in anger at every one of my fellow humans who ever had anything to do with that machine: every worker who bolted every bolt in place, and aligned every tube, and welded every panel, and polished every surface, and every quality control manager who tested every function, and every salesperson who ever touted this "product" here and there and everywhere, and every manager who banked the profit, and every one of the back-room staff who drafted the design and printed the plans and accounted for every sale and filed every invoice and answered every phone-call of enquiry and fixed every IT problem and every security guard who patrolled the premises and locked the gates and protected those "products" and every delivery driver who drove those machines to their destination and every installation engineer who fixed it all up and checked it all out and made sure it was all fit for purpose and switched it all on... and walked away, leaving behind the hum of the metal machine, ready for murder...

Every one of them knows what it is for, and every one of them chooses to take part, chooses be in amongst it, putting their hands it, meddling their minds in murder... every one of them had a choice, and every one of them chose mass murder...

I do not know how anyone can do that.

But what I do know is that that bull who died was truly worthy of his life...

THE DYING AND THE DEAD

I see the dead.

There is always the dead, the dying and the dead.

With my eyes wide open, I see the dying and the dead.
With my eyes screwed shut, I see the dying and the dead.

At every turn of my head and twist of my mind, I see the dead, the dying and the dead.

At every tick and tock of every clock, and every bump of the beat of the heart in my chest, whether I walk or run, or sit and rest, with every inhale and exhale of every breath, there is always the dead, the dying and the dead.

I see them, the dying and the dead.
I see them all, and my soul explodes.

When I see you, I see too the dying and the dead.
When I talk to you, I'm talking too to the dying and the dead.
When I sit down next to you, I'm sitting too amongst the dying and the dead.

I'm all mixed up, with the dying and the dead.

I'm in amongst them all, and tears implode at the back of my eyes and run down my insides, a flood inside my body, and my body drowns.

I am not waving, I am drowning, and I am not laughing, I am crying, and I am not smiling, I am screaming...

I am here and I am there, but it does not matter where...
because everywhere
I am

I am
covered, smothered, buried… with the dying and the dead.

It's who I live with, the dying and the dead.

Whatever I do and wherever I go, and however I may try and not see
and not hear and not know
I know
And I know that I must know
that I must be true
to the truth
and I must be true… to the dying and the dead
and so I see and I hear and I know… the dying and the dead.

I will say to everyone, "Do you see? Do you see? Do you see … the dying and the dead?"
I know that not everyone, really not anyone, practically no-one
Sees… the dying and the dead.
So few see any of them, even one of them,
Let alone the billions of them,
The billions and billions of them,
All of them… the dying and the dead.
None of them seen, any of them, any of the dying and the dead.

I see them and I do not want to see them
Not as the dying and the dead
I'd rather see them
All of them
As the living and the loving
But that is not how it is for me
It is not how it is for them

So what I am stuck with
What they are stuck with
Is me seeing them
Only… as the dying and the dead.

So what clings to me, lingers on me, crawls all over me
swarms all over me and overwhelms me
Is this:

the onslaught of the rolling, tumbling, broken, battered bodies of the dying and the dead, every second, every damned second, every sick and stinking, dirty second I see thousands and thousands, and thousands more ripped and bloodied bodies surging towards me in a torrent of violence, wave after wave of smashed heads and shattered bones, and burst flesh and torn eyes and mouths, scarred and charred faces and bloated, corrupted corpses cracked and crushed in a furnace of hate, a fire of horror that flames out of control in a boiling, seething sea of agony. The acids in my stomach burn and turn in a twist and thrust of dizzying lurching and churning from one horror to another horror, a scream to a scream, a cry to a cry, life and death mashed in a crash of blood and bone obliterated and dissipated in the blood-red channel that hurtles from vein to vein, vessel to vessel in my shivered, curled-up body that squeezes itself into a ball of despair and pain, saturated and sunk in a pool of misery.

It is what I see. The dying and the dead.

I close my eyes and the world murders me with its cruelty.
I open my eyes and the world kills me with its hate.

But I am made born by the dying and the dead
my body is fused from the swollen mass… of the dying and the dead

my throat is filled with the bloody foam that flowed out
from the death shout
that blew out
from the mouths of all of the dying who were made dead

I am the murdered. I am the dead.
I am alive
with the noise and the fury
the rictus of agony
sheared from the flesh
of a trillion souls
severed from life,
life ripped out… from the dying and the dead.

I am the life of the dead
made to live again
in a rage of resurrection
a hundred trillion bones stirring in the soil
breaking through the bloodied earth
a billion fingers and toes and paws and hooves
surging upward from the mud
reaching out for the sky and sun
reaching for light and life
reaching out not to be… the dying and the dead.

With every agony I see
with every sight of every horror, from which I do not turn my eyes,
with every howl of every pain, from which I do not close my ears,
with every smell of every murdered body, from which I do not hold my nose,
I will raise my voice in defiance of my humankind

and I will tell the dirtiest truth
and I will not spare the sensibilities of my delicate fellows
and I will not lie
and I will not lie
and I will not lie
and I will not shy from the outrage that is thrown against me
for the temerity
to tell the pity
of the trillions slaughtered.

I will annihilate the smile
Of those whose bellies swell
With the stuffing of meat and dairy and egg and fish
A bloating that grows only from the violation
Of the body of my Mother Earth
A sick lust sucking
life from the living,
An orgy of violence.

Breaking the silence, I speak the sound of billions.

I see the dying and the dead. And then I speak.

The dead speak when the word is told
the sound of the truth unbound
unwound from the lie that has tied the earth to a past whose time has passed.

Even as I drown, crowded out by the billions of the dying and the dead
I speak the truth.

A LIFETIME LOST IN A MOMENT'S GOODBYE

In only a moment a final goodbye is said, but in the eternity that remains the pain lasts through every minute and hour, every day and year, every blink of the eye and every dream in the night, every second of silence and every thought that catches the heart; it is pain, always. Death moulds the mood and shapes the sound of weeping, as tears fall and the voice cracks in a sob that is folded into a shroud that wraps around a mind saddened and dulled by a loss that can never be unbroken.

I am broken. I am lost. It is that pain of bereavement, again, that defies any smile and brutally presses down upon all imaginings of a peaceful, contented bearing of that journey undertaken along life's crooked paths and shadowed alleyways. I stumble heavily, wearily, to muster, barely, another tired step, just a step into a deeper darkness, the starkness of a soul stripped of light.

It is that pain of bereavement, again.

On Friday 9 November, 2012 one of my finest, most amazing friends, Sammy, died. Sammy was an extraordinary person, a cat with whom we shared our home for over 17 years, from 14 August, 1995 when she first entered my life with the most remarkable wide eyes, a blaze of curiosity and intelligent wonder at the world around her. We gave her the freedom to be in our home, and we gave her love, and in return she gave us love and a delightful lightness of joy that made our hearts dance.

So Sammy, you see, had been with me since way back when, when I really began to try and "grow up" (it's been a long, arduous and yes, futile attempt) and came with us into the first home we ever bought, a flat in Woodford Green, Essex and how my memory is still amazed by her antics in those early days as I walked to the bedroom to catch her climbing the wallpaper and hanging by the ceiling, looking down and around at the land below, and how she showed her cleverness and deftness as she unhooked the catch from the windows and sought to turn the handle to let herself out – and curse that lack of an opposable thumb that thwarted her ambition!

So many years ago, and in so many years there was always Sammy and she came along with me with every turn of my life, into that three-storied home in Romford, Essex – so different to the flat! – with its multiple staircases, and Sammy's careful consideration of every room to find the right spots to turn in a circle and fall contented into a ball of sleep. And then of course, only last year, already 16 human years of age, Sammy came along to another home, my home now, way over in the Northern Ireland countryside, such a long way for an Essex girl to travel from her natural home! But home is what Sammy made this space, even with its big expanse of garden and lawn, which Sammy would patrol with regal authority, and again she took her time in allocating the correct location as her definitive sleeping spot, finally deciding upon the blankets at the back of the airing cupboard in the family bathroom, warm, cosy, and absolutely and only Sammy's place, and so, of course, the door was left open twenty-four by seven, for Sammy to come and to go as she pleased.

The door is closed now.

I have had to say goodbye to Sammy, my special friend. She was not, of course, to me a "pet", nor an "animal companion", she was, utterly and completely, a friend and one of the finest friends I will ever have the pleasure to know. Sammy was a remarkable friend because she did not care for my weaknesses, my failings – so abundant and so apparent – and the errors I made. Sammy never did lay low my soul with a look of disappointment, disapproval or outright irritation, aggravation or overt disgust because of an unintended ill-judged manner or word or deed, as did and do so many of the humans that I know – friend, acquaintance or neither, it does not seem to matter. Sammy cared for me, and loved me, and comforted me anyway.

Sammy did not mind whether I lazed in pyjamas on a Sunday and neglected, quite deliberately, to shave or comb my hair; Sammy came and sat by me anyway. Sammy did not tire of me after I had tired from a long, difficult and awkward day at work (most days, then); she came and sat next to me anyway, and comforted me in that moment with a reach of her paw and a purr and despite all of the stress, the despair and the sadness pressing on my heart from the sharp angles of life, in that corner, in that space, with Sammy on the arm of the sofa, there was a contentedness, a peacefulness, a comforted warmness that softened my heart and eased the strain that stretched and pulled my mind this way and that and that way and this; a moment to savour, always, when there was a Sammy so close, and she purred, and one could feel the purr through the stroke of the hand below her chin where the fur was so white, so pure, so soft.

Through so many things, so many moments, so many twists, disruptions, distresses, disasters, and the odd triumph and success, there was always Sammy. And first thing in the morning the first call would always be Sammy, poised, sat so elegantly and tidily, but ready at the first footstep she heard to let loose that wonderful, long meow, to let us know, oh yes, it is now breakfast time, surely it is now breakfast time! And if Sammy ever was impatient with me, it would be only in my tardiness, and yes this is my fault entirely with responsibility accepted absolutely, at not being eager enough to bring out another tin quickly enough for a second (or maybe even third!) breakfast! But then Sammy would be fine, and could wander at leisure to find again a favoured spot to curl into a round, warm sleep...

And in the sleep of death my Sammy must now rest for all of time...and I have lost her and the heartache is all mine.

It is only my selfishness that begs for her to be with me, sat next to me, and purring with her outstretched paw ready to clench those claws into a sharp reminder for me should I dare to stop stroking her fur too quickly... Sammy has lived her life now, and all of her days were days of love for her, from that first eager-eyed moment of connection to that last moment only two days ago when I looked into her eyes and saw myself reflected in her eyes one final time, as those bright, amazing eyes darkened for an eternal sleep.

My life has darkened now, and no number of happy memories or joyful reflections will or can completely cover that wound that remains with the loss of such a beautiful friend but I must take refuge and, I guess, some comfort to know that, despite my legion of weaknesses, that I have had the privilege to be loved by one as wonderful as my special friend Sammy...

SPEECH: TUNBRIDGE WELLS VEGFEST, 2011

Note: the following is the text of the speech that I gave at the TW VegFest event in Tonbridge Wells, England on Saturday 19 November, 2011.

From childhood's hour I have not been
As others were; I have not seen
As others saw; I could not bring
My passions from a common spring.
From the same source I have not taken
My sorrow; I could not awaken
My heart to joy at the same tone;
And all I loved, I loved alone

Those words of course are the opening lines to Edgar Allen Poe's masterful "Alone", one of the finest, most lyrical short poems of the 19th century. I sometimes feel, as someone deeply committed to the protection, the welfare, the rights of my animal companions in this world, that I am somewhat different, somewhat... alone.

It is only when coming to an event such as this that one realises that... I am not alone, that... we are not alone... we are not alone in the universe, there are other, similar life-forms just like us out there... there are, in fact, lots and lots of us but even so, our differentness is often exaggerated by the indifference of a society that refuses to play its part in the beautiful drama of compassionate living.

Here are but a few telling tales from my own recent past. Last year when the football World Cup was on in South Africa, a few of us decided to go to the pub after work to watch one of the games – 16 of us went in total. As it was after work, people wanted to get some food as well; 15 of us ordered a burger and chips. I didn't order the burger; I didn't even order the chips – they looked a bit rank to me! I subsisted that evening entirely on the nutrients to be extracted from a large number of bottles of Peroni, and I think that I did rather well really... but the point was made, that I was the different one...

At Christmas time, we had a party at work and much was made of the catering that was going to be provided for us – on the evening there were great long tables filled with food, people eagerly picking at the goodies on offer... except that there was nothing there for me. One of the catering staff came over and said, "Oh – you're the one. Your food is out the back, I'll go and get it." Apparently I was the one... but not, unfortunately, in the same way as Keanu Reeves in *The Matrix*... back she came with a plate, looking quite pleased with herself. I took the plate and looked at... well, some soggy green things (it was difficult to tell exactly what they were) not so much drizzled but drowned in oil, limp leaves hanging over the edge of the plate, looking for all the world like the melted clocks in Dali's *The Persistence of Memory*, except that this was no work of art... my mate sniggered and snorted as he drank from his beer and yes, once again I was the different one...

A few years before that I was working at a major investment bank in the City of London and as an investment bank they of course had great wads of cash to flash around spending it on whatever they liked. This was before the credit crunch... but I find it interesting that following the credit crunch they've ended up with even more cash to splash now for failing than they ever had when they were apparently succeeding... such are the mysteries of global capitalism...

Anyway, back then the bank decided to throw some cash down at the lower orders who worked there, such as myself, and they sent us on a ridiculously expensive three-day residential training course at a terrifyingly posh hotel out in the Kent countryside... I'm sure this hotel had never had to put up with the likes of me before and if I hadn't have had my company pass with me I'm sure I'd have been shot at the gates as a peasant intruder... but I *did* have my company pass so there was nothing they could do about it and they had to let me in...

Our training was during the day and all very boring but it was in very fine, oak-panelled surroundings, every detail a deliberate expression of a place luxuriating in its own exclusivity and opulence. But it was in the evening, at dinner, that the hotel really wanted to impress.

From early evening drinks we were ushered through to the dining-room, a space perfectly dressed in exquisite finery, the other guests already making delicate chinks of sound as cutlery met china under the murmur of soft conversation... a piano player made gentle tones at the grand piano... a full grand piano, no baby stuff for this place. We were seated at a long table for the eight in our group, plus our two trainers. I had, of course, explained my dietary needs to the hotel beforehand – as a vegan one learns very quickly to seek to pre-empt any major confusion at the mere mention of that apparently alien-sounding word... vegan. Even so, when the *hors d'oeuvres* were brought through mine was a piece of a fish... I explained this problem to one of the waiters who said, "Oh you're a strict one?" before taking it away. Maybe I didn't want a starter anyway.

Then the main event. The main course. This was where the chef was going to demonstrate his creative brilliance, his culinary genius... and this was full silver-service.

We each had a waiter dedicated to us with the maitre d' in full command of his staff. Each of the waiters stood at our side, holding the silver platters in their hands, the silver domes sparkling in the evening light. With a nod the maitre d' gestured to the pianist who paused his playing, the room fell silent and the waiters placed the platters before us. A moment to savour as we waited for the revelation of what was in front of us. With an orchestrated wave of the maitre d's finger the waiters reached over in perfect synchronisation and lifted the silver lids – my colleagues to a one "ooh-ed" and "aah-ed" and "wow-ed", gasps of delight as they looked on in wide-eyed wonder at their plates. I looked at my... risotto in something less than wonder. "Is that it?" one of my colleagues said as she gazed across at the sorry-looking damp rice splodged on my plate. What could I say? At least the chef had managed a vegan risoto. But they feasted well, my colleagues, that evening on their varieties of so-called "game", the chef's speciality, naturally, the hotel's speciality, naturally, and I was once more "the one"...

The second evening we had the same service, the same dedicated attention to our needs, the same sliver platters, the same nod to the pianist, the same ritual with the team of waiters, the same revelation of the chef's virtuosity and remarkable talent... and I had the same risotto. And I saw the same, pained sorrowful looks from my colleagues.

The final evening after a third day's training, and for the last time the ceremony unfolded as before, the maitre d' ushering us through to the dining room for one more meal... one more example of the chef's magnificence, one further chance to sample the pleasure of his genius; one further pause by the pianist as the waiters raised the polished, silver domes one last time and once more the same "oohs" and "aahs" and "wows" from my colleagues and, oh yes, once more the same risotto for me! Once more I was singled out, I was different, I was alone.

I complained of course although the hotel was completely unconcerned; they make plenty of money by filling plates with plenty of so-called "game" birds, reclining afterwards in the rich rewards from so much praise from so many well-fed, well-satisfied guests.

I mention these incidents not because I felt bad about any of them, not because I felt embarrassed by what happened, and not because I felt that I was in any way wrong for being "the one", for being "singled out" in that way... on the contrary, the very opposite was true then and is still true now...

I seriously could have cared less about being "the one", and I would only have preferred more "ones" to make us into a many... but I was fine without the burger and chips in the pub that day, looking around the table and seeing their hands greasy with the stain of flesh dribbled with oil to burn away the blood; I was fine, really, with those limp leaves at the Christmas party – how could I ever enjoy a party, a festive occasion, if I had corpse parts on my plate? And I was massively unfazed by the pained looks of my colleagues in that hotel as they looked sadly at my plate, and I looked at them and saw their cheeks fat with the torn shreds of the violently slaughtered, their faces reddening and bulging with the stuffed remnants of an eviscerated life.

They may have laughed and joked at the table, at the party and in the pub but when I smile I do not have the tattered flesh of the slain hanging from my teeth, my skin does not ooze the rotten grease of death and when I breathe I do not exhale the swallowed scream of the viciously killed.

There was nothing wrong with being "the one"... but the one thing that is wrong in all of this is that it is the wrong way around – it is the one who rips into the bodies of the dead who should be singled out; it is the one who demands that others die for his or her gratification who should be the one who receives the quizzical, confused glance as we ask, "But why would you want *that*?" and it is the one whose pleasure is found in the sufferance and destruction of the weak and undefended who should feel isolation from his or her peers, the silence that folds like a shadow that comes from being the odd one out.

There should have been fifteen in the pub that evening who were uninterested in any flesh-based burgers, the Xmas party should have been heaving, swinging with the many who could eat whatever they wanted from the long tables, crowded with vegetables, fruits and all manner of non-animal cuisine, and below those silver domes should have been riches aplenty for those whose appetites are sated not by blood and death but by the plant-based offerings of a world of food bursting with goodness, and so they would have been if that chef was worth even a fraction of the cost of a meal held under the glittering light of the chandeliers in that dining room.

So why is it not the right way around? Why is it so wrong?

Because we are led to believe lies. The world is warped, the truth is twisted, the facts are falsified, and the lies are laid out before us for our delectation and consumption – if we choose the lazy way and ask no questions, challenge no assumptions, and suppose that every presumption is promoted for the best of intentions, for the noblest of reasons, with everyone's best interests at heart.

No. This is a dark heart of corruption and distortion; the truth is crushed and lies roll over us; we are led to believe not only that animal body parts and their secretions are essential to human health – despite the irrefutable scientific evidence that disproves this categorically – but also that it must be so hard to live as one who has no animal products in the diet; people are made to feel that it's just too difficult to change, that it's just so hard to adapt to a life free from meat and dairy.

We should not be surprised that this is so. The animal farming industry is worth billions of pounds in profit and those companies – whether producers, distributors or retailers – engaged in "feeding the masses" have a vested interest in everything remaining the same, in keeping the population pacified and docile, the mass of humanity leaning backwards, eyes rolling, tongues lolling and mouths agape as tons of rubbish are poured down their throats. But we don't have to take their rubbish, we don't have to fill our bellies with the bloody remains of the cruelly killed, we don't have to stain our lips with the stolen milk of worn-out, run-down traumatised cows bellowing for their calves, now lying dead with a bullet in the head, shot within hours of being born.

We don't have to do any of that and stopping doing it is one of the easiest things we can do... as well as one of the most profoundly compassionate and beautiful acts we can ever perform.

All that we have to do is to see them, those farmed animals, and see them all for who they really are, and see ourselves for who we really are and then to just modestly adjust our behaviours and live our life slightly differently, so that we can live a life whose every moment is devoted to compassion. This is all that we have to do, to adapt to a life of kindness and consideration for others.

We are an adaptable species. We can adapt to anything. You'd be surprised what people can get used to, you would. It's amazing really, our ability to adapt. There were men, and it was only men, who were taken as prisoners to Auschwitz-Birkenau in the Second World War and were forced to "work" in the murder chambers and crematoria as what the Nazis called Sonderkommando, a "special" team whose task it was to remove the dead bodies from the gas chambers, remove any gold teeth and jewellery – including intimate examinations for any hidden items – and then burn the bodies, either in open pits or in the crematoria. Often, these men saw and had to deal with the bodies of their families from whom they had been separated only hours before – and now they had to destroy them, utterly and completely. Some of those men "worked" in that horror, that abyssal nightmare, for months even in some cases years.

Even under this most extreme of psychological tortures and trauma they survived, they maintained their decency and their dignity... they... adapted. That is a testament to their courage, the strength of their humanity and their determination to bear witness to this most grievous of evils. But they adapted.

All that I ask is that we all adapt to soya milk instead of cow's milk, adapt to tofu instead of ham, adapt to... letting other lives live. I ask only that we all live without the factory farm with its cages and chains, live without the weekly livestock market selling animals to their death, and that we all live without the slaughterhouse as the backdrop to our daily rituals, its walls running with blood, spilt just for us.

We can have *Weetabix* for breakfast instead of sausages and bacon; we can have pizza, curry, burgers just the same... just without the animal pieces, and we can have life all around us not death in us and surrounding us.

We can so easily live in a way that harms no-one, that causes no-one to suffer, no-one to feel pain, no-one to die, to lose their life just for us. We can live and we can know that everyone else lived and no-one died because of us... no-one was shot because of us, no-one was stabbed in the heart because of us, no-one was anally-electrocuted because of us, no-one was kicked in the face, and punched in the eye, and beaten on the head and burned and scalded, and yelled at and cursed and hated and pushed and pulled and thrown and... no-one screamed in pain because of us, no-one bowed their head and cried and died just because of us...

And we can live so well!

There's a reason why heart disease, and diabetes, and obesity and dementia and cancer and so many other desperate afflictions are so rare amongst those who have no animal-based foods in their diet – certainly when contrasted with the meat-eaters in our society. Even taking everything else into account – lifestyle, exercise, age, gender, ethnicity, family history – all of the medical data all indicate that a plant-based or vegan diet is not only a healthy choice but the healthiest choice...

It allows us as human beings to live long and healthy lives, with a much, much lower risk of so many diseases that terrify so many. It is not inevitable that 1 in 3 of us must contract cancer as is suggested by so many cancer charities; heart disease is not an inevitable fact of life that can only be held at bay at best by surgery and a lifetime of popping pills; we do not have to spend the majority of our later years debilitated, in chronic pain, with worn and diseased bones, bereft of energy, vitality, the very life sapped from us even as we live... and wheeze and stagger, bent-double towards a cold, early grave.

The one who is considering, but hesitating, about whether to make that choice and absent all animal products from their life – from their food, their clothes and furniture, cosmetics and household products, should ask themselves the simple question – what's the worst that can happen?

Will their arms fall off? It seems unlikely. Will their eyeballs boil in their heads and explode outwards in a shower of tissue and membrane? That's not expected to happen. Will their stomach erupt in a spasm of fiery rejection of fruits and vegetables, and be ripped asunder in a bloody horror of self-evisceration? That's doubtful too.

The worst, the very worst that can happen is that going shopping might take a bit longer as they scan the ingredients list of items on the supermarket shelf... that's how *bad* it will ever get...

Now what's the best that can happen? The person will feel healthier, more full of energy, and will know that their new diet is one that is most definitely more friendly to the environment, knowing that the precious limited water and food available on Earth is not poured into the mouths of livestock animals but is still there for the billion humans who are desperately parched and hungry. And they will know too that they are not responsible for any pain, any suffering, any violence, any cruelty, any beating, any bloodshed, any killing...

They will know that they are living a truly compassionate life, one that respects all life, one that cherishes life, one that really offers hope to those who hunger and thirst in our world, and offers safety and sanctuary to those who deserve our mercy, and protects and cares for the natural world, that safeguards the rainforests, the mangroves, the coral reefs, the rivers and seas and oceans, the savannahs and the forests, the fields and the wetlands, all secured for future generations to treasure the richness of the variety of life lived therein, and one that offers care and kindness to those who are undefended, that looks after the weak and the fragile, a life that expresses love in fullness and without hesitation, concession or compromise, a live of love lived completely and absolutely, a life of goodness, decency, kindness and compassion offered to all without exception... a long, healthy, wonderful life of joy and love...

That's how *good* it can be.

And we can all do it. We can all live that life. The power is ours, to change our lives and the lives of so many others.

We do not have to wait for anyone to tell us what to do; we do not have to wait to be given permission to do what we want to do; we do not have to wait to change the world. We can do it now.

We are often made to feel powerless, by lobbyists, by Governments, by big business, but they're wrong – they don't own this world; we do. They're not in control; we are. They don't have the power; it's ours. In truth, they're running scared from us, terrified that we won't show our loyalty by always shopping at the same supermarket, always buying the same brands, always voting the same way... if we take away our loyalty, if we refuse to buy into what they want us to do, then there's nothing that they can do about it... and they know it.

They want us to feel weak, but we are strong; they want us to feel helpless and hopeless but hope is ours to offer and help is ours to give. They want us to feel that we can change nothing, but we can change everything. The power is ours; we are in control – of our destiny and the destiny of those billions of others in our world... and we can change the world... by thinking differently, by acting differently, by choosing to live differently, we *can* change the world.

It doesn't matter that we get "singled out", that people regard us as "the one", because we're the ones that are taking a stand, we're the ones that are making a difference... and we are the ones that the world has been waiting for!

CALL TRANSCRIPT: EVIDENCE OF TRUTH

Operator: "Operator. Which emergency service do you require? Police, Fire, Ambulance?"

Killer: "What? Er, Jesus. Police! Send the fucking cops! There's been a murder here! A fucking big killing! Send ambulances too, send fire, send everything. Send everyone! Send the fucking lot!"

Operator: "Okay sir, just stay calm, and..."

Killer: "Stay calm? Stay calm?! What the fuck? Do you even get it? You're asking me to stay the fuck calm, when I'm standing in this shit! Just fucking deal with this!"

Operator: "Okay sir, we'll get all the help that you need, but I also need you to help me. Please tell me your address."

Killer: "What? My address? My home address? I'm not at home! Jesus fuck."

Operator: "That's okay sir, please tell me where you are now."

Killer: "Right now I'm standing in shit. It's like I just woke up from some kind of weird daze, and now I look around – and fuck! There's blood everywhere! Just fucking blood everywhere! I look at the walls and they're covered in blood, the floor's covered in blood – god shit, my clothes, my hands are covered in blood. It's just fucking blood. It's fucking everywhere. Just do some shit here, ok? Get me the fuck out of this shit!"

Operator "Okay sir, please be calm and..."

Killer: "Fuck off, I can't do calm! Not with this shit everywhere! How the fuck can I be calm! Do you even get what the fuck I'm looking at, what the fuck I'm standing in here?! Have you got one fucking clue how many fucking dead bodies I'm looking at right now?"

Operator: "Then please let me help you. Tell me where you are and we'll get help to you."

Killer: "I'm fucking at work. I'm in fucking work. And it stinks of shit and piss and blood and death, just death, fucking death. I'll tell you where the fuck I am, I'm fucking in hell. It's shit, it's fucking shit. There's so many dead bodies, so much fucking blood, so much fucking violence. Jesus, it fucking hurts to have my eyes open and see this shit. Fucking get me out of here!"

Operator: "Is there anyone else with you? Is there anyone alive there?"

Killer: "Huh? Uh, yeah. There's others, co-workers. They're still here."

Operator: "And are they okay?"

Killer: "Yeah, they seem okay. But I'm not sure they're seeing what I'm seeing. I can see this shit, and it's a fucking nightmare. I've got to get the fuck out of here – you've got to help me!"

Operator: "Do you know who did this? Do you know who committed this crime? Are they still there?"

Killer: "Yeah, we're all still here."

Operator: "We?"

Killer: "We did it. I did it. Me and my mates. Who work here. We did it! I did it! We done it all. Fucking stabbed them like shit. Fucking stuck them, stuck them all, fucking knife in the heart, in the face, the fucking back, just where the fuck we want – just fucking killing them, killing them all."

Operator: "Can you please tell me where you are?"

Killer: "Just doing my fucking day job – I'm at A&Z Meats, the slaughterhouse. And I'm gonna be sick, I'm gonna fucking throw up."

Operator: "The slaughterhouse? Okay. Sir, tell me – the dead bodies that you mentioned?"

Killer: "Yeah?"

Operator: "Are you talking about the animals that have been killed?"

Killer: "Damn fucking right! It's just fucking horrible!"

Operator: "Have any people been hurt?"

Killer: "Humans you mean?"

Operator: "Yes."

Killer: "No."

Operator: "Is this some kind of joke? Are you playing stupid games with me here? You phone up, going on about murder and you're telling me it's just a bunch of animals! What is your problem? This is ridiculous, and a waste of my time!"

Killer: "Fuck you! Do you not get it? They've been fucking murdered. They hurt. They feel. They suffer. They know! I know now, I get it now, I've fucking woken up, I can see the shit I've been doing day after fucking day. It's a fucking horror story. It's sick. We're sick. You're sick. Our world is fucked! What fucking job is it that I pull on my overalls, pull out a knife and stab hundreds of screaming animals in the heart hour after fucking hour, day after fucking day? For what? For fucking what? Hey, you eat meat, right?"

Operator: "Yes of course, and ..."

Killer: "Then you're a fuck. And you are fucked. You want me to stand here all day fucking killing so you can eat some shit fucking sausage for dinner? Fuck you! Just fuck you! I ain't doing this shit. I can see now. This is fucked. I hear them scream. I'm the one who gets up close and fucking personal and I feel their breath, and I see their eyes, and then I get their blood all fucking over me when I stick them. What the fuck was I doing? What the fuck kind of hell hole shit is this? Fuck it. No! No! Not having this fuck. I'm out of this shit. Send the fucking cops, send a fucking ambulance, send a fucking fire engine. Arrest every fucker here for being the fuckers that they are. Arrest the fucking managers sitting on their lardy tub fucking arses counting fucking money while I drag fucking corpses around, and arrest my shitty co-workers getting their fucking kicks beating and punching the animals screaming in fear and sheer fucking terror. Then smash this fucking place, tear it the fuck apart, pull it to fucking pieces and plant some fucking trees and flowers. Get fucking real. And you, Mr Operator fuckwit, get your fucking skull sorted and deal with the shit you've put me through. Cut the shit out, lose the fucking meat, and eat some fucking greens you dumb fucker. You asked me if any 'people' got hurt, well yes they did – all those animal people got real fucking hurt, and I'm really fucking hurting, I'm in some serious fucked-up trouble here. I need some fucking major fucking therapy. You any fucking clue what you and all those fucking sausage-eating shits put me the fuck through here? My brain is fucked, my mind is fucked, my heart is in fucking pieces. I need to be fucking sectioned from reality, because if this is reality what I'm looking at right now – rows of ripped bodies, blood everywhere, animals cowering, crying, trembling, waiting for their turn to be murdered – and it is reality, because I'm standing right in the shit of it, then I want the fuck out of here. Send me a fucking ambulance and lock me the fuck away somewhere! Got that?"

Operator: [silence]

Killer: "You still there Mr Operator man?"

Operator: [silence]

Killer: "You fucking fuck! Put the phone down eh? Too fucking namby fucking pamby to fucking listen! What a shit. Too fucking scared! Well, I'm here, I'm in this shit, I do this shit for you and every other fucking meat-munching fuck-wank out there in that shitty fucking fucked-up world and you're all too fucking scared to listen, too fucking spooked by the fucking truth, don't want to know, don't want to give a shit. Tuck it all away, keep the shit out of sight, shove it out of town, and send sad fucks like me into fucking hell to do the fuck for you. Fuck that! Fuck it all. I'm a killer, I'm a murderer, and this is murder, this is a fucking nightmare, this is a fucking crime, the biggest, baddest, nastiest fucked-up crime of them all, the vilest, meanest, sickest, most twisted, violent, bloodiest, shittiest crime of them all. And I'm done. I'm gonna wash the fucking blood off my hands. Now what the fuck are you going to do?"

THIS CONCERNS EVERYONE

(Written in homage to and with the greatest respect to the late, wonderful Adrian Mitchell)

I swallowed the truth one day
And ever since then
I've talked this way
So soak my mind in butter
Tell me lies about the food we eat

You heard them all screaming in pain
And told yourself it was just a game
So smear my face with cream
Soak my mind in butter
Tell me lies about the food we eat

You shove the cows in, and yank the organs out
You slice and dice the corpse, the hate is never in doubt
So drown my lungs with milk
Smear my face with cream
Soak my mind in butter
Tell me lies about the food we eat

Where were you when they were ripped open alive
Ignoring all their cries on a summer Sunday drive
So stuff my mouth with eggs
Drown my lungs with milk
Smear my face with cream
Soak my mind in butter
Tell me lies about the food we eat

They pick the piglet up, and smash him on the floor
They stamp his face with boots, and find it such a chore
So fill my ears with entrails
Stuff my mouth with eggs
Drown my lungs with milk
Smear my face with cream
Soak my mind in butter
Tell me lies about the food we eat

They scream for life until their dying breath
So you can sit comfy and dine on death
So clog my heart with meat
Fill my ears with entrails
Stuff my mouth with eggs
Drown my lungs with milk
Smear my face with cream
Soak my mind in butter
Tell me lies about the food we eat

SPEECH: AWAKENING TO ANIMALS 2012 (THE POLITICS OF COMPASSION)

This is the text of the lecture that I delivered at the inaugural international "Awakening To Animals" conference, held over the weekend of 17-18 March, 2012 in the beautiful setting of Lake Windermere, in the Lake District in Cumbria, England.

The Politics of Compassion

"I will let loose a thunderstorm of love, a downpour, an outpouring of compassion, a torrent of hope for those who thirst for freedom, bringing forth a raging flood to wash from the face of the Earth all the vanities and cruelties of humanity, to leave thereafter and ever after a sea of calm and peace whose islands are oases of comfort and security for the weak and the undefended. Now is the time to let fall the first drops of rain to herald the changing of the Earth."

We live in a time and a space when humanity's cruelties are all too apparent; at every turn of the Earth and dawning of each day yet more evidence is made apparent by the light of the sun of humanity's hatred of the natural world and its billions of inhabitants, doomed to suffer lives of brief but abject misery and pain. And yet, we know, it can, so easily, all be so different, if we choose... to look and to think and to feel just a little bit differently. And this truth which is within us is made all the clearer when we take a step backwards and outwards from ourselves.

This image you see on the screen is, perhaps, the most truthful and, perhaps, most beautiful, of all photographs ever taken. It is certainly the most distant. This photograph was taken in 1990 at the request of the late astronomer and populariser of science, Dr Carl Sagan. The spaceship Voyager One, which had been launched in 1977 to survey and photograph the Jovian planets, was at that time on the cusp of crossing the boundary of the solar system, some four billion kilometres from Earth. Dr Sagan thought it would be a good idea to send a request out across the reach of space to Voyager One for the craft to turn around briefly and take a photograph of the place from which it had come, our small world Earth, before continuing on its journey across the vastness of interstellar space.

This is the photograph. From four billion kilometres away it shows our world lost in the remoteness of space, floating as a dust mote against the backdrop of cosmic night, and caught by chance in the thin stream of sunlight from its parent star, our sun. More eloquently and more simply than any other image ever could this photograph expresses the utter sequestration of our world in the awesome immensity of the universe and life's utter isolation in the protective envelope of one small, pale blue pixel. That is here, our Earth, with warm oceans and blue skies, a globe of safety set against the black death and deep cold of darkest space.

Our home is our protection and we would do well to protect our home. And though our current obsessions with profit and possession, domination and conflagration seem instead to set our course on self-destruction, there are many who recognise the urgency for a change in direction, a rethink of our attitudes and actions, a re-examination of our intentions. An overhaul, long overdue, of all that we think and do, a revolution in the head, and a revolution in the heart. To embrace change is to embrace hope, and to have hope is to make possible the future we intend, not the future with which we must contend.

We can have the world we want. I demand the chance to create the world anew. As with all of us here today, my motivation is empathy and compassion, the desire to reach out and connect with all others with whom I share this small world, and embark on a life dedicated to concern and consideration to the needs of others. Life's journey should be a journey undertaken in company, a united community walking in concert with each looking out for his or her neighbour, offering support, safety and security for all, as we find expressed so often in the selfless, altruistic natural world which is anything but "red in tooth and claw". Our civilisation is expressed through our social and political structures, the systems we elaborate to define our relationships with one another.

For too long those political, economic and social orders have failed even to deliver a civilisation worthy of the name. They have not been designed to promote community cohesion or to provide comprehensive protection and welfare for those most in need but instead have been deliberately constructed to bestow excessive luxury for the few, a self-appointed, self-aggrandising elite looking out only for their own interests, securing for themselves an ever greater proportion of the world's gifts at the expense of the many, condemned to subsist on an ever smaller share. The strong dominate, demand all for their own satisfaction and indulgence whilst the weak and the undefended must scratch and scrape for the fractions of the morsels tossed down from the heights of luxury onto the dirt paths the poor must walk in search of something, anything, just a little more than nothing.

Thus do our political systems corrupt whatever civilising tendencies we may naturally hold in our hands and hearts, debasing our desire to treat all with equal consideration... the organisation of our politics and economics has been co-opted by the greedy and the selfish, the brutal and the cruel, whose disinterest in the welfare of others is the mirror opposite of their interest in acquiring ever more for themselves.

We know that that is not good enough, not good enough by any stretch of the ethical imagination. And we know too that however little attention may be given to the needs of the poor and the vulnerable in our human community that it is our non-human animal friends who are exposed most shockingly to violence and viciousness, the devastation and destruction of their lives.

That is why I chose to enter the political arena, as stained and soaked with corruption as it is, to stand up and stand out and offer a new voice that spoke for those whose world was least regarded, whose bodies were dismissed as mere commodities and whose minds were shattered by the unrelenting terror of their daily trauma. On their behalf, I stood for election for the political party Animals Count on two occasions, the European elections of 2009 and the General Election of 2010. For the first time in UK electoral history, there was a candidate promoting an animal protection manifesto; a credible, practical manifesto whose central concern was to promote not only the welfare interests but the rights of non-humans. And so I said what needed to be said.

And no, I didn't win ... on either occasion. Of course I didn't win on either occasion. The UK's electoral system is utterly twisted and attuned to the interests of the major political parties only, with money the essential source of electoral success. With neither the cache attached to the "Big Three" parties nor substantial funds from a Central Office to bankroll relentless PR opportunities we knew that we had to run a campaign whose intent was not necessarily to emerge in first place on election night but to take our animal protection manifesto into the heart of the political process. And so the measure, we believe, of our success, was positive coverage and interviews in the national press and on national television, together with the distribution of leaflets and other materials into hundreds of thousands of homes.

This meant that when I took part in hustings events with other candidates I was able, time and again, to bring the discussion around to critically important topics such as climate change, the trashing of the earth by factory farming, the destruction of the seas by the fishing industry, the vile horror of the slaughterhouse, the damage done to human health by a poor, animal-product diet, the valueless cruelty of vivisection, the shame of a nation that claims to love animals and then murders them by the billion. The other candidates, of course, just wanted to point score, preferred playing the game, mocking the electorate with every false word they uttered. For the general election, a few weeks before polling day, I remember waiting to be interviewed for the BBC's "*The Daily Politics Show*" and I was in the room with Michael Gove (Conservative) and Chris Huhne (Liberal Democrat) – both had just been on screen and tore into one another mercilessly and yet now, in the room afterwards, they laughed and joked, remarking at what positions they could each get in the event of a Conservative-Lib Dem coalition. Electoral success, for the professional politician, is all about power, influence and prestige.

And so why engage at all with the political system? Because I believe that the time is right to offer something different, something genuinely alternative to the tired, discredited and dysfunctional credos peddled by the major parties, who offer only sectarian self-interest to their targeted constituency.

They do not speak for all in society but only for their own closest social neighbours; they do not listen to the needs of all in society but deliberately turn their ear from the voice of the many whose needs are greatest; they do not see the results of their policies but close their eyes to the stain of blighted communities. They... do... not... care.

The inevitable effect of the politics of self-interest is a rip in the fabric of our society; isolation replacing solidarity, the group turned against itself.

There is a fracturing of community spirit, a breakdown of social cohesion and narrow self-protection that sets neighbour against neighbour. All of which leaves our non-human animal friends utterly cast out and ignored.

The late American philosopher Terence McKenna wrote about what he called "the balkanisation of epistemology", the falling apart of a once common world-view shared across society, the disintegration of a united perspective, ruptured instead into what was described as the "curse of relativism", an atomisation of ideas, the rise of individualism over communitarian support, the absence, keenly felt, of a mutual understanding of one another's needs.

How then to create coherence from a cacophony of clashing philosophies and ideologies? I believe that the answer lies in peeling away the layers of discord to uncover our commonality, all of those things we share equally with one another and yes that of course includes the things we share with those multitudes of non-humans as well as our fellow humans. When we return again in our mind's eye to Dr Sagan's famous photograph of the distant Earth and look upon this shared world from the distance of deepest space we know that whatever differences between us all that there may be are trivial to the point of irrelevance when contrasted with the thoughts, feelings and values, wants and desires, interests and concerns that we all share.

The method that we use to unveil the underlying truth of the interconnectedness of all lives and the intrinsic value of every life is to bring to bear upon our reflections the twin pillars of the evidence of science and the principle of natural justice. It is what we uncover through the scientific method that leads us ineluctably to the full measure of an ethical life. And it is by being honest about and trusting of the data we deduce through the application of science that connects us most fully to the world as it really is. That is why my political manifestos have been constructed upon a solid foundation of the results of scientific enquiry; the ethics of my politics shot through with the truth revealed by research from around the world.

The scientific method, properly applied, represents the most successful mechanism we have yet devised to draw out from the natural environment that surrounds us the fundamental attributes of all who rely upon that natural world for their survival. And what the evidence tells us, clearly, dramatically, incontrovertibly, is that all living beings have rich, complex psychological and emotional lives as well as a physical presence, a profound sense of who they are, and a desire – a genuine, absolute desire – for freedom; all animals whether human or non-human, are motivated by the same wants and hopes, the same determination to live out the fullness of their lives according to their own interests and needs.

Thus does this scientific data inform our morality – because we, as humans, know the richness and wonder of the lives of our non-human friends in this world, then we must – if we are to be moral, if we are to be ethical, if we are indeed to be civilised – we must give full and complete attention to, and recognition of, and total support for, the rights of those non-humans in our world, and offer to them the same protection we would afford to our human fellows, absolutely and without hesitation and without concession.

Though we are always human, we fail to be humane unless we grant to all the right to freedom, the right to protection from violence and coercion, the right to life. If we want our society to be a just society then we must acknowledge the reality of the data uncovered by our science and connect the truths thus revealed to our moral systems. In such a way we therefore see that the parallel towers of scientific enquiry and natural justice loom large over our lives and we stand in their shadow, knowing that it is for us to live up the principles of truth and justice, not for them to be bent down and corrupted to match our opinions and prejudices.

It is our courage, our determination, our integrity and unshaken focus on rights for all that will allow us to create the world we want to see. Every day I remind myself of these great words of Mr William Lloyd Garrison, written in 1831 in the first issue of his magazine, *The Liberator*:

"I will be as harsh as truth, and as uncompromising as justice. On this subject, I do not wish to think, or to speak, or write, with moderation…I am in earnest – I will not equivocate – I will not excuse – I will not retreat a single inch – AND I WILL BE HEARD."

An American in the early 19th century, Mr Garrison was a tireless campaigner against slavery, calling for the "immediate emancipation" of all slaves – no half-measures, no concession – and also devoted huge energy to the women's suffrage movement. Where he saw injustice he demanded justice. He knew, it was obvious, that no slave should be held in bondage, that the very notion of slavery was an abomination; and he knew too that no woman should be made to bow to any man; he knew, it was obvious, that all humans were and should be equal, that no mere appeal to skin colour or gender, or any other attribute, could legitimise the debasement of one before another. How absurd it is for us now to try to turn our thoughts to the mindset of the racist or the misogynist – what an affront to all decency to imagine that one's sex or skin pigmentation should decide our status in society, should be a factor in our freedom...

Mr Garrison never lost sight of, never for one moment forgot, that his motivation must be justice for all, rights for all, and he would without fear or concern set himself against any and all whose opinions were simple prejudice and arrogance. He always was as harsh as the truth and as uncompromising as justice.

In this was he was joined by a near contemporary, Mary Wollstonecraft, the author of "*The Vindication of the Rights of Woman*", a revolutionary in her time and an inspiration in ours. She too saw the connection between the rights of one group and the rights that should therefore be afforded to all others. Her anger at the treatment of animals spilled out in a letter after reading about the killing of some horses by King George III, as she wrote:

"*I cannot bear an unfeeling mortal. I think it murder to put an end to any living thing... if it has pleased the beneficent Creator of all to call them into being, we ought to let them enjoy the common blessings of nature, and I declare nothing gives me as much pleasure as to contribute to the happiness of the most insignificant creature.*"

In her defence of rights and her call for justice she showed no fear and refused to be cowed by the bile and vitriol her words inspired in those who preferred an unjust world, a corrupted and prejudiced society. Status, influence, power – all of this meant nothing to William and Mary, they were going to stand up for justice anyway. Titles and power disappear in a puff of irrelevance when it comes to the defence of rights, when it comes to us to be as harsh as the truth and as uncompromising as justice.

No deference to authority will suffice and no docility in the face of forces ranged against us could ever be acceptable. When we know, as we do, that all animal lives, whether human or not, should be lived within the protective shield of the right to freedom, the right to protection from harm, the right to life, then we know also that which we must say and that which we must do, if we are to uphold the twin standards of scientific integrity and natural justice, if we will indeed dare to be as harsh as the truth and as uncompromising as justice.

Where we see injustice we must make the demand for justice. Where we see violence, cruelty and killing promoted and promulgated in our society, normalised and justified because "it's for entertainment, it's for research, it's... for dinner", there we must step up, step out and stand against that violence and killing, on every corner, down every street, throughout every day – we make ourselves heard. We do not equivocate or prevaricate, we do not excuse or make apology, nor ever sanction or endorse ourselves those horrors done. We know the truth; therefore we tell the truth. We know what justice means; therefore we demand that justice be seen.

This is the courage of the one who will not be a bystander. We know the violence that exists in our world, the brutal cruelty that crashes down upon the gentle minds of our non-human animal friends, captured and confined on our farms and slaughterhouses, our laboratories and zoos and I do not need to dwell on the desperate details here today. But it is appropriate to restate our commitment not only to defend what is right and just but to make the world right and just.

It is a famous saying, many people repeat and repost it daily on Facebook and elsewhere on the Internet, and I am sure it is nothing new to anyone here today to repeat once more Mahatma Ghandi's oft-quoted demand to us to, "Be the change you want to see in the world." Those are fine words, all well and good, but not really ultimately good enough and we must be bold and go further and be not just that change we are so desperate to see but be also the revolutionaries, the William Garrison and Mary Wollstonecraft of our day, to create that world, to remake and remould the world in the shape of justice. We cannot exist only in a bubble, living principled, decent lives of honesty and integrity if we are also in near-isolation from our peers, invisible to society, our thoughts and deeds unknown and unacknowledged, impacting no-one, changing nothing.

Justice is not a philosophy, it is an action. It is always an action. Justice fails when inaction takes precedence, when fear of challenging authority, fear of "stepping out of line", fear of the consequences of raising the voice, of raising the hand to say "No", takes over and the body remains still, inert, the throat mute, the mind silent and one becomes, a bystander.

We are all too aware of what happens when people become bystanders, when fear or self-interest wins and justice loses. We know what that looks like, we know the inevitable destination to which the undefended are dragged, the shape at the end of the line for those who would not be saved. This place, this space of abyssal horror, Auschwitz-Birkenau.

This is the spur of the railway line that took hundreds of thousands to their immediate stinking, filthy deaths in the murder chambers of this, the most technically advanced of the Nazis' Vernichtungslager or extermination camps.

Auschwitz-Birkenau and the other camps, and the death pits where two million were shot to death, were permitted to exist in the world because too many stood on the side of the road and watched and did not act, or stayed away and did not act, who refused to move and refused to speak. We are far enough away from the events now and we know enough now about those events to know that there was no inevitability to the construction of the extermination camps, that Nazi Germany did not represent some all-powerful, terrifying monster of invincibility. But for six million or more, the bystanders won, and the world was left to wonder...

What horrified the world then and still wrecks our sensibilities now is not what transpired at Auschwitz but what transgressed, a wholly new order of criminal violence and hate, an utter inversion of morality, described then as the Anus Mundi, the arse of the world; beyond the gates, once passed through those gates, was a different moral universe that permitted, endorsed and acted out a meticulous slaughter of the innocent in forensic, technical detail, an unparalleled opportunity for the full force of hate to take its vengeance against the broken bodies of the weak and the undefended.

It represented such a horror that many thought the world could not recover, would never be again what it was before. The German cultural historian and philosopher Theodor Adorno was so shaken that he said that there could be "no poetry after Auschwitz", as though language had to collapse in on itself, overwhelmed by the crushing gravitational force of the brute fact of Auschwitz.

Theodor Adorno was nearly right, he just used slightly the wrong words; not his fault, he was trying to articulate an unimagined reality of cruelty. Of course there was, is, poetry after Auschwitz, and extraordinary poetry too, some of it reflecting even on Auschwitz. Poetry lives on. Poetry must be, as John Keats tells us, "Beauty is truth; truth, beauty" and there is still beauty in our world despite Auschwitz. What Theodor Adorno should have said was "no poetry *in* Auschwitz"... for all of the things we now know of what happened beyond those gates, all the stories and the testimony that has come down to us, tell us that there was no poetry in that place – there were many things, writings and drawings, photographs, love even on rare occasion, but no poetry; the truth of Auschwitz is not a poetic truth, it refuses poetry for it refuses beauty, it is ugly only, a thick, ugly scar on the tortured face of humanity.

I have spent time on this subject today because it is of utter relevance to our world, our present, for we have our own Auschwitz-Birkenau, our own extermination camps... the factory farms and slaughterhouses, the research laboratories, that condemn the innocent to lives of sufferance and then, their murder.

The slaughterhouse is our Anus Mundi, our dirtiest stinking hole of horror, our nightmare of crime. There is too no poetry in the slaughterhouse, no words of beauty that could ever be composed in the stun room, the sticking room, the death pit. Beyond the gate of the slaughterhouse is a different space, a transgression, a wholly-other moral order that twists and corrupts the structure of the mind, that permits, endorses and allows to be acted out, that unleashes acts of staggering cruelty and viciousness by the powerful against the weak and the undefended in forensic, technical detail, the machinery of murder meticulously arrayed against the innocent, the bloody precision of unrestrained hatred.

We pass through those gates into a morally-inverted deathscape, a space deliberately arranged for nothing but violence and killing, where all common measures of decency and goodness, justice and mercy, kindness and compassion, must fall and fail, are revoked and replaced by the standard of the brute and the bully, the cowardly killer who stands tough, armed with weapons of mass destruction, over the shaking, terrified body of a small animal and even then the killer kicks and beats, punches, stabs and spits, screams and only then delivers the fatal shock.

The Nazis may have lost the war but they tore a scar in the heart and they won over the mindset of humanity. How else can we adequately describe the reality of the slaughterhouse? We live in a Nazi world.

Much criticism has been levelled at those who have described this direct connection between what the Nazis did then and what we do now, great thinkers such as Isaac Bashevis Singer, and great writers such as Charles Patterson, but they are just choosing to be honest, and what else would we ask for from our thinkers and writers but to be honest? Do we not now prefer a William Lloyd Garrison and Mary Wollstonecraft to their many contemporaries whose minds remained closed and who spoke only lies and denied the truth?

Who will be our hero and heroine? Will we want the bystander to be the standard-bearer for our time, to represent us on the field of history? As dawn breaks open a new day, who do we want to see – William and Mary or the unknown man and woman skulking in the shadow, eyes looking down not wanting to catch the notice of anyone, never hearing, never seeing, never feeling?

Auschwitz still exists as a museum, its murder chambers detonated and destroyed, silent witness now not only to mass murder but to the mindset of the bystander, the betrayal of justice. But our slaughterhouses are anything but museum pieces, many of the killing lines roll 24 hours a day, ever more victims are drawn and dragged daily through the gates to a filthy, stinking murder only hours away. And we have to do something about it.

If we are going to be awake to animals, then we must be awake to the demand to act now to put a stop to the most egregious, most pointless and most cruel of humanity's evils: the destruction of trillions of land and sea-dwelling animals every year to satiate our hunger. This is something that is not only a despicable act but also a most foolish act given all of the scientific evidence that describes us so clearly as herbivores, a naturally plant-eating species for whom the consumption of the flesh and fluids of animals represents an act of health-damaging self-harm. When we recognise the evidence of science we of course recognise the kinship we have with those with whom we share much of our evolutionary heritage, our biochemistry and our physiology; we recognise that, like them, we survive best on plant matter, when we eat what is natural for our kind – the fruits and vegetables, nuts and seeds which are ours to take in our share from nature's garden.

This not only aids and strengthens our health but also impresses upon us an ethical focus to regard and treat other species in a way that is also natural for our kind. We do not have to kill to live; we never have to kill; our life can be lived in fullness and richness and we never have to kill; none need ever die for us to survive. We can live and live well and never kill. Never, ever kill.

This is the greatest, grandest truth of them all. This is the simplest and most special truth of them all. This is the truth that can set billions free.

And we who have acknowledged the truth must be the ones who will not be bystanders. We who are awake to the lives and minds of those other animals with whom we share our lives must be the ones to awaken the imagination, the heart and the soul of all in society to the richness and joy of this most noble of truths – that we can all live lives free from causing suffering and pain, free from the destruction of other lives, free at last from the enslaving lie that lashes us to a bloodied past. Free to walk into a future in which love and compassion are the inspiration for our society's daily acts, a drama whose story is one of kindness, selflessness and common consideration for the needs of all in our world.

We can have the world that we want. We can and we must politicise love and compassion, embed our economics with the full strength of the moral life. It is possible to articulate the vision of a society where the "drive for growth" is in wisdom and emotional maturity not the acquisition of yet more material possessions, where we place our faith and hope in empathy and not in money markets. A world in which wealth is calculated according to the richness of our inner lives not the flaunted luxury of consumer items, to be discarded and replaced with the later, greater, newer version the moment they are possessed.

It is the politics of compassion, predicated upon a solid foundation of scientific evidence, which can allow us to reshape the world for the benefit of all. Currently, our overriding political and economic doctrines are skewed towards self-interest only which not only leaves much of the human community on the outside looking in at the feast on the table, but also defines our non-human friends as mere property, pure product, commodities only with no safety or sanctuary from the barbarity of industry which seeks only to render them from living, feeling beings into parcelled, packaged remains on the supermarket shelf. Because of this legal positioning of the status of non-humans as functional objects that can be possessed and then destroyed with impunity, then wherever we position ourselves on the political spectrum – whether right or left or some imagined, idealised centre – is of no consequence to those non-humans, for the spectrum itself has the shade of ingrained prejudice that traps in the glare of its dark light all species other than human in a nightmare of annihilation.

Our politics must be informed with something other than an historical allegiance to a left or right ideology whose mantras have never provided what was promised, have never delivered on what was claimed and have never granted and will never grant to the most vulnerable the protection they deserve which the strong can afford to give.

The politics of compassion offers us all the solution which is so desperately needed. By taking full and honest account of what the data from our sciences tell us, and imbuing our philosophy with the principles of natural justice, we derive a politics of rights that is awake to the reality of the needs of all in our world, irrespective of species as well as, of course, irrespective of gender or skin colour, and which recognises the intrinsic value of all lives and the utter certainty that every life is unique, precious and worthy of being provided for and protected from every persecution.

The politics of compassion are ours, and ours to deliver to the world.

We can regard again Dr Sagan's extraordinary image and see, with our hearts, that that faintest of small, blue globes is all that we know and know too our role in securing a future upon its rocky and watery surface for all who cling to those rocks, swim those waters and ride the winds that roll the air.

Every hope for every living being is ours to offer. Every gesture of kindness is ours to express. Every expression of kinship is ours to give. Every gift of love is ours to grant. Every chance of life is ours to award. Every place of safety is ours to provide. Every embrace of protection is ours to bestow.

With our hands we can shape the future. With our eyes we can see those who need, with our ears we can respond to their cries, with our voices we can make them heard.

With our minds we can offer rights, and with our hearts we can offer love.

With our love we will recreate the world in the image of love. It is love that will define us and it is love that will inspire us to break open the heavens to let loose that thunderstorm of love, that overwhelming outpouring of compassion, offered to all without exception. Because we are alive, we are awake, and because we are awake, we are love. We are awake to animals because we are alive to love.

ANIMALS RIGHTS EQUALS HUMAN RIGHTS EQUALS RIGHTS FOR ALL ANIMALS

I stood before Justice. I looked. I could see no dividing lines, no cuts that separated one part from another, there were no half-measures, no half-empty cups, there were no dark corners hidden from the light, no shrouded folds that masked one part from any other, no boundaries or borders that I could see or sense, there was no edge. Justice spoke with the noise of rolling thunder and the wind of her words shook the foundations of the Earth – "I am whole. I am indivisible. I am what I am and no-one can set me against myself. I bow to no-one. No-one can corrupt me or change me, twist me or turn me – I am absolute, I am immaculate. I am justice."

Justice exists or it does not exist. Those who take justice seriously, and who are determined to rise to the challenge of extending the reach of the light of justice to shine ever more brightly in this dark and damaged society, must know that justice can only work when it is complete. Justice demands the truth and justice demands no compromise. Justice flourishes only when it is not perverted by our inadequacies or any moral distortions borne of our chauvinisms. Justice either is or it is not.

Those of us motivated by a demand for justice for those billions of non-humans in our world – the animal protection "movement" if we can give it a name – who suffer such extreme prejudice, exploitation, brutality, violence, hatred and fatal cruelty, must also be motivated to ensure that all prejudices and violence that arise from the bigoted attitudes and actions of one group against another persecuted group are erased from our global community. Anything less does not satisfy the demands of justice, and anything less than justice is an absurd waste of time and effort.

Some in the animal protection movement claim that so long as one is driven by a determination to end the enslavement of non-human animals, then it does not matter what views and opinions one holds with regards to other humans (and we know that many are in positions of exploitation, legalised discrimination and on the receiving end of great violence and often fatal harm). The suggestion made is that, so long as one does *something* to help non-human animals, then it matters not at all if one is at the same time also racist, misogynist, disablist or homophobic (and so on). This is a ridiculous assertion that not only strains credibility but is a venal debasement of the meaning of justice. Justice does not sanction one prejudice when contrasted with another; justice is not satisfied with one bigotry replacing another; justice is not served when the chauvinist is regarded as a worthy ally in the fight for freedom for our non-human friends. It is a mockery of justice and confirms only that injustice will continue to dominate our society.

The proposition that prejudicial views expressed by someone towards others is of no consequence so long as that person is working towards ending non-human animal exploitation acts only as a sop to the bigoted, providing them with a false sense of entitlement to ridiculous, discredited and obscene opinions whose only intention is to perpetuate discriminatory, exploitative, antagonistic and downright contemptible attitudes towards their own target group – whether based on gender, sexual orientation, race or other arbitrary characteristic that rankles with their unformed, squalid reactions to those whom they perceive as "different" and therefore unworthy of the respect, tolerance, compassion and decency that they expect to be granted to themselves. Prejudice of any kind is a sickness of the mind. The cure is social justice, expressed fully and completely, without compromise or twisting or hiding of the truth.

The promotion of animal rights is one of the most astonishingly difficult prejudices to overcome, given how deeply embedded it is in the cultural structures and legal and political systems of our world. We all have to work extremely hard to ensure that those who currently hold the opinion that non-human animals are unworthy of the full protections of the law and the extension of love and compassion to them and the proper attention to and satisfaction of their needs must be mindful that, if we then at the same time hold opinions contrary to the basic principle of social justice (that no-one should be discriminated against based on some randomly-chosen trait) it makes us look ridiculous, foolish, very stupid, and frankly really pathetic. It is difficult enough to find an outlet in the traditional media that will present animal protection issues in a favourable light without us making it so much easier for those who oppose our compassionate views to hold us up to the cold light of public scrutiny and say, "Look! Look at your animal rights zealots! Fanatics all of them – racists, homophobes, women-hating! Look and see! Aren't they stupid?!"

Yes, it is stupid. It has no place in a tolerant, empathetic and compassionate animal protection philosophy. Animal protection is a matter of pure social justice. Non-humans are exploited against precisely because society currently tolerates and condones the commonly-held prejudice against them that they are unworthy of proper protection, based purely on their species membership. To counteract that bigotry is to strike at the heart of what and who society is for. It was a long and extremely hard struggle to fight against previously embedded bigotries in our society – whether slavery, the exploitation of women, the criminalisation of homosexuality – but over the course of recent centuries we have begun to emerge from those darkest days, and the majority now recognise, and our laws largely endorse, the common view that all humans are indeed equal. What an absurdity to set ourselves against someone based upon their skin pigmentation, their gender or preferred sexual partner!

One day it will be the case that our society will also recognise the absurdity of setting ourselves against our fellow Earthlings based only on their species membership, the count of the number of their legs or whether they have fur ... but to get there we have to be smart, we have to be intelligent, we have to be consistent in our philosophy, we have to be articulate in our denunciation of the prejudice meted out to our non-human friends. We have to be respectful, compassionate, wise and loving. And the baseline for that is a complete rejection of all forms of prejudice. The determination to secure protection for non-human animals stands absolutely side-by-side with securing protection for all humans – it is the same thing as human rights. Animal rights includes human animals as well as non-human animals. Justice exists for all or it does not exist for any – because then injustice is sanctioned and can always be extended to include more (after all, if one group can be prejudiced against then why not another?).

If we want justice to be on our side, then we have to love and to love all; we have to express respect, tolerance and compassion towards all, no exclusions, no divisions. Justice demands it and justice bows to no-one.

Trust in justice, trust in compassion, trust in love.

THREE JOURNEYS

What is a journey? Here is a snapshot of a moment earlier today, about three journeys…

The first journey is my own. I caught a taxi at my house in Ballinderry Upper to take me to my local train station, Moira, for the next rail service into work in Belfast, Northern Ireland. As I got in the car, the taxi driver told me about another journey. He was just starting his shift and was making his way from Donaghcloney to Magheralin when he came upon a car accident that had just happened; that is the second journey. Like other motorists he stopped and pulled over. The car was on its side, and the driver (the only person in the car) was a large man, who looked to be in his 30s, and was trapped in the car, wedged in and unable to free himself. One of other motorists had already called for an ambulance and had been advised that the driver should be left where he was – no-one was to try and move him. The driver was dazed and confused, and looking pale; there was a clear head injury and blood stained his forehead – but he was conscious and able to talk to the other motorists.

There was, of course, great concern for his safety and well-being and some of the other motorists had switched on the hazard lights of their own cars to warn other approaching drivers of the danger ahead. They were talking to the injured driver, and letting him know that the ambulance and fire services were on their way, and he would be freed in no time. The taxi driver, seeing that everything was under control, saw that there was nothing more that he could do and so continued on his way, and a few minutes later here he was, telling me all about what he had just witnessed.

He was telling me how this had shaken him up a bit as we drove up to a junction and then paused to let traffic pass. As we waited there (it's a busy junction) and he continued to tell the story of the car on its side, I noticed one of the vehicles passing us was a large green lorry, and this is the third journey. The lorry was heavily-laden with the "goods" it was carrying and I could see the "products" it was transporting because of the spaces between the wooden panels on the side. This was a "livestock" lorry, which was crowded with cows, all on their way to the slaughterhouse. As the lorry passed, it was as though time slowed and I was able to see the cows inside looking out at the world speeding past, and I can see vividly even now, in my mind's eye, as one of them looked directly at the taxi that I was sitting in, and it seemed as though one of them looked straight at me, and the moment froze as I saw her eyes seeing me... and then the lorry continued on its way, and shrank from view. Through all of this the taxi driver continued telling his tale of the second journey; he didn't even notice the livestock lorry, it was just another vehicle to him, and nothing to be concerned about anyway, that was just normal, he was much more concerned about what he did see – the large man wedged into his car, titled on its side. He continued to tell that story all the way to Moira station.

Three journeys. In my journey, I just got a taxi and then a train and got to work, nothing got in my way and the worst that happened was that I arrived in work. For the large man's journey, all of a sudden his world was on its side, and he was in pain and discomfort, but he had a lot of people around him, all focused on helping him and wanting to support him – that was a few hours ago and so by now he'll be free from his broken vehicle and no doubt in hospital where care and help will be given to him until he's well enough to walk out and get on with living his life. For the cows' journey, they have no doubt arrived now at their final destination, where they will be greeted with shouts and screams, being prodded, pushed and beaten to make them move forward to their place of death. They will smell what the place is all about, they will see what it all means, they will hear the screams of their fellows, and they will tremble and shake in fear. Their journey will end with their violent death. How many – apart from me – even noticed their journey, or even cared what that meant for them? There was no-one to fuss around them to see if they were okay, because no-one cares if they're okay, because no-one wants them to be okay – they want them to be dead.

Every day there are thousands of journeys just like that third journey and no-one even notices, or pays attention – deliberately fatal journeys that we all accept with not even a shrug of the shoulder, it doesn't even register, we don't even see those journeys, we don't even see those trembling, fearful beings inside those lorries ...

We just don't see because we just don't care ...

SPEECH: ARAN, DUBLIN 2012

This is the text of the speech that I gave at the national Animal Rights Action Network (ARAN) demonstration in Dublin, Ireland on 25 August, 2012.

"We're the mad ones, the ones who are mad to live, mad to love, mad to be saved, desirous of everything at the same time, the ones who never yawn or say a commonplace thing but burn, burn, burn like fabulous yellow roman candles exploding like spiders across the Milky Way."

That's us!

I steal those words of course from the beat generation writer Jack Kerouac, because I believe that they precisely, perfectly encapsulate who we are and the place and the space in which we find ourselves. Seemingly isolated, stood separated from the mainstream of society that meanders around us, we are utterly, irresistibly drawn not only to animal welfare, not only to animal protection, but to animal rights, and animal rights comprehensively expressed, defined and enshrined in law, as we ask that everyone in our society – whether human or non-human – be able to live out the fullness of their lives, in safety and security, free from all abuse, exploitation and violence, the cruelty of the zoo and the circus and the racecourse, the laboratory and the farm and the slaughterhouse banished for all time.

It's not a lot to ask for.

And it is what we should ask for, it is what we must ask for.

A lot of people, we know, think us hysterical, sentimental, impractical and unreasonable, or terrorist or extremist, hard-line, hard-core, hard-wired to zealotry, in a restless, ceaseless rollercoaster ride of provocative, emotive action, reaction and counteraction. In equal measure, it seems, we agitate and irritate, and our words, our demands, resonate in the ears of everyone around us, in the world that is not mad, apparently, that surrounds us.

But I am glad to count myself amongst the mad, because this does not make us bad... it makes us right.

When we petition, lobby, clamour and call for change, for real change, to change the world... it means we're right.

Not for us the shadows in which to hide, the side-lines on which to stand, bystanding as the world goes past, because we choose to stand in the bright light of justice, burning with the fire of compassion and driven within by the unstoppable power of love. Of course we are right.

No matter that we may be mocked, ridiculed, scorned, derided and castigated; we are right anyway. Words of criticism and opprobrium are as nothing set against the towering majesty of justice, allied to the overwhelming forces of love and compassion, who all are our constant companions. Of course we are right.

And because we are right that is why we stand here today, and that is why we stand firm in our call for animal rights.

We are intractable, implacable in our opposition to all exploitation, resolute and unyielding in our demands, because we know that justice by halves and quarters is not justice at all, because we know that compassion offered only to the few is not compassion at all, and because we know that love denied to the many... is the enemy of love itself.

So we can't be bargained with, we can't be haggled with, we can't be bought with favours or corrupted by empty gestures, we can't be compromised by false promises, we don't collude with cruelty and portion off the rights of one against another, we don't offer a sacrifice of lives to secure a benefit for ourselves, we don't bow in deference to authority, or yield to pressure, or acquiesce in the face of injustice... because what we do *is* justice, what we do *is* compassion, what we do *is* love... and love does not fail.

So we do not waver, we do not falter, we neither slip nor stumble but walk strong and determined towards the future that we will make present, towards the world that we know will be ours. Step by step, word by word, action by action we make that world where none suffer because of who they are, because of the species to which they belong, because of the count of the number of their legs, or because of their fur, their flesh, their milk or their eggs, just because they happen to be born a non-human animal and not a human animal. In our world, this world that will be ours, none of that will matter at all... all that will matter is love.

We do not have that world today, and there are so many that we cannot save today. I know that you, like me, have stared into the dark horror of hell, at the blood-soaked nightmare, and heard the cry of agony... but we have not averted our eyes, we have refused to turn away or close our ears, we have chosen to see, and to hear, and to know, and to look through our tears to bear witness to them, those gentle, beautiful ones, and we have chosen to reach for them, to stretch for them, to comfort them and to care for them, to know them and cherish them, and to live our days in memory to them, and to fight for them and those who come after them, to know that the future for them will be that day when we can say, "That day we fought for is today. That day is today. That day is today!"

Because we may well be the mad ones... we are also the amazing ones, the extraordinary ones, we too are beautiful ones, because we're the ones who live moment by moment with passion in our hearts, with justice on our minds, with love burning like wildfire through every vein and every vessel, every muscle and every tissue yearning and desiring freedom, safety and sanctuary for all, compassion to all, love in all its wonder and its glory given to all without exception or selection. That's us!

We're the ones who will make the world what it's supposed to be, we're the ones who will create the world as it was always supposed to be; we're the ones who will give to the world the love that was always meant to be; and we're the ones who will grant the chance of joy and happiness, and freedom and gladness to our animal friends that they always deserved to be theirs. That's us!

We're here today because we believe something, because we feel something, because we know something:

We're here today because we know what tomorrow will bring,

We're here today because we know we're going to win!

REMEMBRANCE OF THOSE WHO PASS BEFORE US

By the grave we weep
In memory we keep
The one who died
For whom we cried

Graves and graveyards, our monuments to the dead, are places that draw us, stilling our minds and hearts, slowing our footsteps as we walk, reverently, in the spaces that run between the stones. The outline of each plot marks the path we can take so that we can avoid, irreverently, treading on the dead. We respect them, those who were here before us and who now lie beneath us in a thick shroud of six feet of earth to protect and secure their mortal remains. Heads, instinctively, bow in their presence, voices soften and quieten, an unspoken recognition of the need for due consideration and honour to be given to these who now are bone only or dust indeed, worn down by the decades, or centuries even, that have passed since their passing, time spent silently in the spot of ground that was granted to their body on a day, long gone, of tears and sadness.

Wherever possible, we leave them be. We can see the graves tilt with the shifting of the earth, lean this way and that, and sometimes fall flat, with the slipping away of years and more years; the stone shows signs of weathering, a cracking and breaking, the lettering – once stark and clear – is smoothed and fades, becomes mottled, harder to decipher, hiding for all time the name of the one who dwells below. But still, we leave them. Still, we respect them. Though no relative visits with flowers or thoughts of remembrance, though the grave is untended and no lamentations take place at its side, we leave them be. This is their body, this is their place, and we honour and obey the respect first accorded to them on that day which dawned with the beginning of their eternal rest.

We believe in them, their inviolable right to be at peace, as we see it, protected from interference and allowed to remain, untouched, to fade from the world. We believe that all of our fellows should be so provided with the thoughtful and dutiful tribute to their life with the quiet dignity of a burial ground, into which, gracefully, gently and with care, we lower their form for a hoped-for, unending tranquillity.

What a shit, therefore, that we discard all concern when it comes to the cow and the chicken and the pig, the sheep, the goat and the turkey. All gentleness tossed aside, all grace abandoned, it is the fist and the boot, the iron bar and the knife that is used to bludgeon the life from them. Regarded as mere product, reduced to commodity, treated as valueless so long as they live, we drag them kicking and screaming into a noisy, dirty, noxious-smelling hell-hole of carnage to kill them as soon as the economic advantage to do so is ours to take, along with their life. There they are punched and beaten into submission, then blasted and stabbed to death, the blood pouring from their hanging bodies. In an unending line of disassembly, the dead are drawn on hooks and pulleys towards workers wielding massive metal tools to tear and rip, slice and shred each body, cutting limb from limb, organs pulled out and pulled apart, the body – rapidly, dramatically – moment by moment disappearing in a frantic weave and wave of blades and chains. Some body parts are meant for preservation, to be diced into small parcels for consumption, but others are destined for immediate discard, dumped into tanks and channels of blood and waste, congealing into a decomposing mass comprising the unwanted remnants of hundreds and thousands of bodies.

No dignity in death. No resting place of peace. No quiet space to fade gently from view. Dismembered, torn apart, ripped asunder, annihilated and eviscerated, corrupted and devastated, the bodies of billions are violated with the grossest of violence that humanity could ever conjure from the filthiest and most callous corner of its mind. For the legion of animals born and doomed into the world of the farm, there is no peace at the end for them, it never ends well, because it never begins well and never is well from the beginning to the end, and after the end, when each one is done to death, then still we unleash the sheer physical force of our viciousness against them, never satisfied until we have slashed them into oblivion, unrecognisable scraps of tissue, dirty lumps of flesh and blood-soaked bone.

There is no remembrance offered and no monuments made to the tens of billions who yearly pass through the fatal horror of the animal farming "industry", and no respect given to the countless lives lived in such squalor and ended with such horror. The land should be covered with individual graves to each individual that ever suffered the nightmare of the slaughterhouse and the indignity of his or her body being shredded and spread across dozens of "patties" and "pasties" and "burgers", mixed with the remains of their fellows, and swallowed into the guts of the greedy and the ignorant. We should raise a monument to each and every one of them. And then, when the land is swathed in graves, and our feet bump, trip and stumble over grave after grave after grave after grave after grave and there is no room to stand because the dead have taken all of the land, maybe then, we may recognise the enormity and monstrosity of what we have done, the full scale of the misery and despair we have shoved under the earth, tucked out of sight, and then, perhaps then, we may step back in shock (and trip and fall over another grave) and yell, "For God's sake, stop!", and then, at that moment then, we may, at last, finally, just... stop.

Until that day I will not stop my demand for it all to end, my voice will not be silent, I will not be stilled. I will not stop until animal farming is dead. And the death of animal farming will not be mourned. I will happily, gladly, piss on its grave...

THE MENTALITY THAT MURDERED MARIUS MURDERS MILLIONS MORE

Written in February 2014 when Copenhagen Zoo killed Marius, a young and healthy giraffe because of 'gene pool diversity' concerns, a killing which received a lot of media attention.

Why do we pity that one who walks before our eyes but are blind to so many others?

The news over the last couple of days has included extensive coverage of the decision by the Copenhagen Zoo to kill Marius, a two-year old giraffe held captive at the zoo. There was a concerted effort via social media to save his life, to no avail, as the trivial reason given by the zoo for killing him was that Marius was 'surplus to requirements.'

The zoo confirmed that Marius was perfectly healthy, there were no concerns over illness or pain that he might be experiencing. He was, they confirmed, a healthy young giraffe. He was simply 'surplus' to need, and the stated reason for him being 'surplus' was that the gene pool for captive giraffes is quite limited (inevitably) and thus they did not want to him to breed with anyone and potentially cause 'problems' for either themselves or some other zoo owner in the future.

Marius could have lived; Marius wanted to live (he certainly did not commit suicide). He died only because the zoo's administrators did not want him to live. They murdered him (how else to describe deliberately taking the life of one who does not want to die?) and, in that, the animal 'welfare' officers who also work at the zoo were fully complicit, providing the means (poison and a gun) and the personnel to kill him.

We should not be surprised. Zoos (and their watery equivalents, aquariums) kill animals all the time. For mere financial reasons they maintain very tight controls over the numbers of animals they hold captive, and seek alliances with other zoos to 'swap' animals and 'manage' their 'collections.' Zoo owners feel that too many animals will pose 'risks' that they do not want to deal with – for example, at the same time that Marius was being killed in Denmark, six Lions at Longleat Safari Park were murdered due to 'excessive violence' (or so the park claimed). The managers further alleged that that the animals displayed 'neurological problems' because of inbreeding, and it is inbreeding that is the connection with the Copenhagen case.

But it is the zoos and safari 'parks' themselves who are the cause of the problem. There are only so many animals "to go around" and who can be permanently confined. With limited to no birth control measures in place, the inevitable outcome is to cause a limited 'gene pool' for producing future generations of captive animals. The direct, deliberate result is that the zoo owners will kill the animals that they do not want, irrespective of whether they are healthy and full of life.

Many were shocked at Marius' deliberate murder, and took to social media and forums to complain angrily about the waste of his life. And quite correctly so. But how many of those who were roused to such anger for Marius also consume the "products" of the meat and dairy industries which daily murder thousands of thinking, feeling beings (no different to Marius) who are also claimed to be 'surplus to requirements'?

For example, the "egg industry" murders over 200 million baby chicks in the UK alone *every year*, simply because those newborns happen to be male – and thus of no "value" to an industry dependent upon the female of the species to labour relentlessly for them to produce the prized possession (eggs) which can be sold for profit at the cost of those animals' lives. These "surplus" animals, just one day of age in the vast majority of cases, are killed in violent, brutal fashion either being stuffed into sacks to suffocate and be crushed to death by their fellows, or dumped onto conveyor belts that draw to them to a "macerator" – a machine that slices and grinds them up alive. The violence involved is horrific. But companies choose to produce these macerator machines (such as KL Products, Ausager and Hawkhead), some of which have the capacity to 'dispose of' (that is, grind up alive) some 40,000-80,000 young chicks *every hour*. In all cases, the lives being destroyed are described as "waste" or "by-product", never as feeling, sentient, sapient individual beings who have only just been born and have barely had a moment to begin to stretch their wings – wings which will never stretch in freedom.

The "dairy industry" too has its "surplus animals", dependent as it is, just like the egg industry, on the female of the species to relentlessly produce their prized possession (milk) which can be sold for profit at the cost of those animals' lives. Male calves born into this industry also have no long-term "value" (they will never produce milk) to the industry and thus they too are regarded as "surplus to requirements". Their fate is to be either shot dead within days of being born or confined for the whole of their brief lives (a few months at most) in tiny crates, unable to turn and indeed barely able to move at all, simply to satisfy the financial cravings of the "veal" industry, which will then murder the baby calf and cut him up to satisfy the gustatory cravings of those who desire the taste of the parcelled flesh.

What this means is that in order for one's anger at Marius' murder to be a meaningful anger, given that he was held captive against his will in the zoo industry, one must also, by sheer force of moral logic, be implacably opposed to the murder of hundreds of millions of other innocent young animals, held captive against their will in the animal farming industries. We cannot weep for one but be indifferent to the other without being guilty of a grave moral error, indeed a hypocrisy that screams out from every egg, carton of milk and slice of meat on every shelf in every supermarket and in every butcher's shop. If those "products" are part of one's regular diet then it is difficult to see how it is appropriate to be angry or upset at Marius' murder whilst at the same time being a deliberate participant in the murder of others who suffer equally and whose lives are ended in violence for naught but the perceived "needs" of a for-profit business enterprise.

Marius' case is desperately sad. What a folly, an absurdity it is to have zoos and "safari parks" (in truth, small fields that in no way replicate the scale of the land over which the captive animals would naturally roam) in the 21st century. The claim is that these places serve to provide education to visitors but countless studies prove over and over that visitors spend mere moments reading and learning and the majority of their time staring and pointing. They learn nothing, not even that the evidence before their eyes confirms that the animals at whom they are gawping and laughing are deeply traumatised and profoundly distressed by their captivity and the maddening, stultifying dullness of the grinding, eventless routine of their daily lives, permanently on display for the humour of tourists.

In any event, the knowledge already accumulated in books and films and shared globally through the media demonstrates that there is no need for any animal to be imprisoned in an utterly unnatural environment simply to satisfy whatever curiosity we may have regarding their habits, diet and sex life. This prurient prying into the hours of their lives is an unwanted and unwarranted intrusion into the privacy that should be theirs, to be expressed in the freedom of their lives that also should be theirs.

A zoo is not only an anachronism, a throwback to an unenlightened age of exploitation, it is a moral outrage, pandering to the base behaviours of an uncivilised society that considers wandering along signposted pathways ("Lions this way!") and staring at the confined animals to be a satisfactory and amusing manner in which to pass a bored afternoon, as people amble absent-mindedly, occasionally stopping to point at the 'funny antics' of the 'funny animals.' And more so the administrators and managers, many of whom are scientifically trained, and who ought to know better but believe that the welfare interests of these animals could ever be served by causing them to be dragged or born into captivity, living the entirety of their lives in abasement and abject ecological poverty, and who can, at a whim, at the discretion and direction of a neatly-attired officer with two eyes on a balance sheet, be deemed 'surplus to requirements' and shot dead.

So too that immense global horror that is the animal farming industry, whose very purpose is always and only to destroy life after life after life, whose functionaries daily perform their tasks of mutilation and destruction with machines perfected for the violent murder of millions of innocents, all deemed 'surplus to requirements.' Such savagery and cruelty, such insensitive butchery, should not exist or persist in any society with even the vaguest claim to civility. Animal farming, that vicious construct to satisfy the casual pleasure to be had from a TV dinner or a quick bite to eat at lunchtime, is itself a zoo, its one exhibit – the whole – is the corrupt and vile mind of humanity at its worst.

If you weep for Marius – and any who are decent and kind will weep for his loss – do not then grab a hold of an egg sandwich to be washed down with a milkshake…

Note: only a few weeks after the killing of Marius it was reported (25 March, 2014) that Copenhagen Zoo had killed four lions – two elderly and two cubs – in order to "make way" for a "new lion" that they wanted to "exhibit". The murder continues.

DO YOU KNOW ME?

The hair on my back is broken because my back is broken. My eyes weep tears because my eyes are bruised. My mouth drips blood because my mouth is smashed. My legs shake because my legs are kicked from under me. My whole body trembles because of the blows that fall upon me from boots and fists and hammers and metal bars.

I die because you kill me.

Did you even notice me? Did you even know that I was there? Did you see me or hear me or smell me through any of the days and nights that I lived? Did your mind even turn towards me for a fraction of a fleeting moment as your eyes fell upon the cut packages of my corpse that lay upon your plate, as the smell of my burnt flesh was sucked up your nose and your mouth broadened into a contented grin? When you cut into that small bit of my body, covered in sauce and flavoured by an array of condiments did you think to stop to picture me whole, complete, as a full body, and breathing and living, standing and knowing, feeling and sensing as I felt the confinement of a cage, the taut pull of the rope that tied me in place, the dull pain of the bruises that covered me left and right, up and down, from the never-ceasing rain of blows and kicks that daily made me shudder in terror and cry in pain, my voice echoed back at me from my fellows who, like me, were stuck, trapped, and suffered just the same as me, and felt the force of the hate that beat against our bodies?

When your jaw was opened in a smirk of satisfaction in the comfort of a prettily-presented table at dinner, and you drew to your mouth the fork with which you stabbed the smallest part of me, and you bit your teeth down on me, and chewed and squashed the tiniest fraction of me, did you pause and imagine me, and consider me as I stood shaking in horror at the gate of the place where they killed me, where they pushed me and pulled me, kicked me and thumped me, and yelled at me and screamed at me, and poked me and laughed at me, and thought nothing of me, as they attached me to their chains and I was heaved forward into their machines, not only their machines but your machines, as those machines fixed me and locked me, pressed in upon me, and held me in a vicious grip as they prepared me, and then finally stood over me, and again laughed at me and in a split second held the bolt against me and blew me... away, blew my brains from me, shattered me, destroyed me, in a moment wiped me... out, killed me and murdered me, ended the days of me, took away me... from me, and made me dead, a thing, a corpse that they hoisted above their heads, and on their pulleys dragged me, a dead me, along the line where they dismembered me, ripped me and spilled all of the blood of me, and trashed me and cut me, tore me... into pieces that looked nothing like me, that obliterated me, made me into nothing as they shredded every last piece of me, and poured bits of me down a drain and other bits of me dumped into bins, and some bits of me they preserved... for you?

And so, did you, at the moment when you chose to chew your jaw down on the smallest scrap of me, did you even think of me? Did you hear me, the screams that I bellowed in the final moments of me, and did you smell me, not the gravy and the sauce but the stink of me and my terror as they yanked me and killed me?

And when you swallowed that small chunk of me, one of the little bits left of me, did you reserve for me, in the moment of your pleasure as my fragment tumbled down your throat, a small glance in your mind to reflect upon me, and who I was and what my life meant to me, and the pain and the fear which never left me but was with me, in every day and night of the life of me, always there pressing upon me and distressing me and terrorising me, all of that which was done to me, did you think of me then and did you notice me?

Or did you not even care for me, even at the moment that you ate me? Did you not even think to think of me, and did you not even think of those pieces of me as being me? Did you know me even as you smiled at me as you cut me, those little bits of me?

And can you not, now, even remember eating me? Did the eating of me mean so little to you that you cannot even think to recall when you ate me? Was I really so nothing to you that you never knew that I was a me and you cannot even now remember cutting the remains of me and swallowing those pieces of me?

What does that make you?

SPEECH: NATIONAL MARCH FOR FARMED ANIMALS, 2012

This is the text of the speech I delivered at the National March for Farmed Animals in Brighton, England, 7 October, 2012.

If not for justice, then for what do our eyes see?

If not for compassion, then for what do our hands reach?

If not for love, then for what do our hearts beat?

Justice, compassion love – these three are what drive and inspire and motivate us as we work tirelessly towards a future free from all farmed animals – where fields have crops and no livestock, where grain is grown for hungry human mouths and the rainforests flourish once more, in a world that is at peace with itself.

Justice, compassion, love – these three are the rock-solid backbone that strengthens our determination to rid our planet of the nightmare of animal farming, the most vicious and pernicious of evils that the crooked mind of humanity has ever made manifest, the worst done by the basest of our desires, a cruelty unrivalled, a wickedness unparalleled, a violence shot through with a hatred unmatched, the shock of the sickness of humanity at war with everything that is good and decent and kind.

Justice, compassion, love – these three are our strongest weapons, our power to overcome the horror, to forge a new world, a force that through our words, our hands, our hearts the truth at last will be told and heard.

For we stand, defiant, with the truth and under our feet, shattered and broken, are the bitter lies of the animal farming "industry" – in reality, a monstrosity of diabolical cruelty, a dark world with no escape for billions of the gentlest, most beautiful of all lives, a black hole of despair and pain, cloaked by the vilest of lies. Because to pocket the profit that flows from the blood of the innocent, the masters of this misery do nothing but lie.

They lie about the human "need" for meat; they lie about the human "need" for milk; they lie about the human "need" for eggs; they lie about the human "need" for "fish"; they lie about "free-range"; they lie about "enriched cages"; they lie about life on the farm, in the sheds, in the crates; they lie about the suffering felt by those farmed from the violence of their birth to the violence of their deaths; they lie about the dirt and the filth and the disease; they lie about the despair, the terror and the madness endured; they lie about the transports; they lie about the slaughterhouse; they lie about the kicking and the beating, the punching and the stabbing, the screaming and shouting, the scalding and mutilating, the hating and the killing, all of the killing, and through it all... they lie.

We... tell the truth.

And this truth that rests in our hearts is the truth of hope offered freely to the world, opening the opportunity of a life lived that is *for* life, that is *for* compassion, that is *for* love. This is the life that truly offers something for everyone, a share for all from the gift of nature's garden, where we take only what we really need and leave alone those innocents who will be free to live their lives in their own way, following their own path, for if animal rights means one thing it is their right to be left alone. To be left free from our coercion, confinement at our hand, free from the violence of their exploitation – free to be the rare and precious and beautiful individuals and personalities that each sheep, pig, chicken, cow, turkey, bull and fish truly is.

We want them to be free because we know that it is not enough to know what one is against, one has to know also what one is for, and we know that we stand for a world with less violence, less cruelty, less suffering, less pain, less waste of our limited land and food and water, less despair, less misery, less hate, less bloodshed and less killing. A world with more kindness, more sharing, more selflessness, more altruism, more hope, more compassion and more love.

Less of what horrifies, and more of what inspires;
Less of what destroys, and more of what creates;
Less of what hurts, and more of what comforts.

Fewer tears of pain, and more tears of joy and
no livestock, no cages, no slaughterhouses.
Anywhere. Ever.

That is our world, and what a wonderful world that will be!

That is what drives our lives, and it is for that world that our hearts beat, and as our hearts beat we do not forget the reason why, so deeply and so badly, we want that world, because:

> between every heartbeat, we hear the sound of the chirp of the newborn male chick, bewildered as he is tossed alive to the sack to suffocate;

> and between every heartbeat we hear the sound of sorrow of the cow, in mourning for her lost son, shot dead in the head at just one day of age;

and between every heartbeat we hear the sound of the cry of the saddened goat, in mourning for her lost daughter, sold to slavery to satisfy a lust for her milk;

and between every heartbeat we hear the sound of the scream of the baby boy pig, fixed upside-down and castrated in full consciousness and no pain relief, his legs kicking in furious agony;

and between every heartbeat we hear the sound of the muffled sigh of the chicken as his legs break under him from his swollen chest and he falls exhausted to die on the filth-stained floor;

but between every heartbeat, our hearts beat faster and faster with the desire for justice to be seen, for compassion to be done, and love offered to every one of these billions of innocents, setting them free from the misery of their enslavement, the cage doors snapped open and discarded, the chains in tatters, the machinery of annihilation pulled asunder as a heap on a floor that will no more flow with killing and the loss of blood.

With our every heartbeat we desire a kinder, gentler, more compassionate world, and with our every heartbeat we bring to pass the greatest revolution in all of human history, and it is we who are on the right side of that history. The future will be what we dream today.

And so today, with every step
always know and never forget
that you are the world made wonderful
and you are the hope and the inspiration for that revolution
for the creation of a whole new Earth

And with every step
always know and never forget

that because of our justice, our compassion, our love we will change the world because we tell the truth, because we live the truth, because we are the truth, because we are justice, we are compassion, we are love!

TOTAL ANIMAL LIBERATION – THE PATH OF TRUE JUSTICE

The Facebook group "Total Animal Liberation" has been established and is publicly open for all to join, and the following represents its founding principles and Declaration.

Animal liberation is a vitally important cause, perhaps the most pressing, the most urgent and most serious rights cause of the 21st century. The exploitation and destruction of non-human animals, involving tens of billions of individuals every year, creates immense suffering, pain and despair through their mistreatment in farming, research and entertainment as well as effecting massive ecological devastation and having a catastrophic impact on human health through the ingestion of animal flesh and bodily fluids, and the absurd use of non-human animal subjects in scientific experimentation.

Animal rights matters.

But let us pause a moment to understand fully what is meant by animal liberation.

We should not forget that humans are animals too, and there are a vast number of commonalities in biology, psychology, language and expression, cognition and emotion and social organisation that we as humans share with non-human animals, and those commonalities are more numerous than any differences which are trivial in nature and extent.

The course of human history has represented a long, hard and dangerous struggle to achieve liberation for all members of the human community, a struggle which is not yet won, despite some of the advances made over recent centuries and the important (but not enforced) propositions enshrined in the 1948 UN Declaration of Human Rights. There are still many hundreds of millions, billions even, of humans who live daily with persecution and discrimination, under threat of verbal and physical assault and even murder, whether by vigilante groups, militias or state-sanctioned and endorsed killing by their own government.

The incomplete emancipation of all humans, the failure to protect the needs of everyone in the human community and the continued expression of bigoted attitudes and vicious attacks against persecuted minorities is a cause of immense suffering, pain and despair, a nightmare of terror and fear as well as bloody violence, cruelty and physical annihilation.

Human rights matters.

It is our contention, indeed it is the foundation stone of our ethical philosophy, that the demands for human and non-human liberation are part of the same struggle, that each represent the same social justice issue and the satisfaction of both is what will make our society, finally, a positive and healthy living space that thrives in harmony with the natural world, in balance with the ecology of planet Earth. If we can neither exploit human nor non-human animals, then we will need to live differently, we will need to live more wisely, and our entire social, commercial, political and legal structures will require a radical overhaul to enshrine the protections of everyone, irrespective of species membership or any other characteristic, ensuring at last that freedom is a road that can be walked by all in our world.

We therefore contend and declare the following:

1. animal rights includes rights for both human and non-human animals;

2. the liberation of non-human animals does not stand in opposition to the liberation of persecuted minorities in the human community;

3. the recognition of the rights of non-human animals further recognises the vital importance of the rights of human animals;

4. there must be a minimum moral baseline to our advocacy, a minimum standard of ethical principle for those who advocate on behalf of non-human animals, and that minimum standard is the complete rejection of all forms of discrimination and prejudice, whether based upon "race", gender, sexual orientation or other random characteristic selected by the bigot;

5. we recognise that all forms of prejudice are philosophically untenable and morally repugnant;

6. the emancipation of non-humans should ensure that there should be no diminution of any rights granted to human animals, and that all should be granted the legislative and political safeguards necessary to confirm their welfare and freedom from persecution, discrimination and arbitrary harassment, physical assault and murder. The reverse, of course, is equally true and of equal significance and importance;

7. advocacy for non-human animal liberation should not seek to ride roughshod over the hard-won, long-fought for protections now offered (however incompletely) to persecuted minorities in the human community and neither sanctuary nor endorsement within the animal liberation movement will be granted to those who hold opinions contrary to the basic principle that all humans deserve equal respect and recognition of their welfare interests;

8. it is entirely appropriate that we choose to focus our energies, attention, resources and efforts on the liberation of non-human animals, who face a dire situation of institutionalised, normalised and legalised persecution and killing on an enormous, global scale;

9. we further recognise, however, that others will advocate on different matters of emancipation and that there should, therefore, be common solidarity between all advocacy groups who all wish for a more humane, peaceful and tolerant world;

10. advocacy for non-human animals is an enormous challenge in a social landscape that has regularised the violence and murder committed against those non-humans who suffer so desperately, and thus our advocacy must make all efforts to ensure that it is expressed in a meaningful, mature and positive manner that helps others in our community to understand how rational, reasonable and sensible is the emancipation of non-human animals and how it does represent simply a logical and prudent extension of rights granted to human animals (and not in opposition to it).

We must all understand that advocacy for non-human animals demands great determination in the face of hostility and adversity, a huge commitment of time and intellectual and moral energy from people across the human community who recognise the extreme importance of social change to eliminate the persecution and annihilation of these billions of pain-sensitive, sapient, sentient individuals ... and the best hope for our success is to adopt a position of justice for all whose underlying moral principle is equality for all, expressed through compassion and love.

Animal liberation for all matters. And it matters equally to all who are persecuted. Animal liberation for all is our best hope for a better world.

HOLDING UP MIRRORS IN A HALL OF SHADOWS

The following is something I wrote way back in the day when I lived in Chennai, India for a while and I just found it again. Unfortunately, it's all still true...

Chennai, India – November 2001.

Here I am without a mouth; I am mute; I have no voice. Why?

What I am about to write is all absolutely true, and it shouldn't be.

I had some free time the other day (I don't have much of that here!) so I decided to get out of the apartment and go for a walk; this was a different kind of walk to those that I am used to in the delightful woods of Epping Forest, or down and through the leafy, really quite elegant streets of Woodford Green, Essex. This was a walk somewhere different: here, this place, Chennai, India, in the midst of people living in deplorable debasement.

There was myself and O, a New Yorker who lives in the same apartment as myself. We were on a casual stroll, that's all, and then we decided, on a whim, to go off the main, so-called "highways" and turn into the streets that so many only turn away from. We went down the winding, cramped lanes to see and to know the truth of where we live, because mostly here we live in rich seclusion, surrounded by a falsehood: we live in a bubble, a bit of the first world that pretends that the rest of the world really does not exist, that those "other" people really do not live, or if they do, do not live like that.

So we walk down these streets. The homes, such as they are, are dilapidated beyond repair, would never be repaired, would be condemned in another place; they have no running water, no electricity, no gas, and there are only a few, modest possessions within. Yet the residents are the lucky ones, for many others have no home at all, they live on the streets by the river (a sewer really), on a rubbish tip (literally), because there's more nutrition to be had on a rubbish tip by a sewer than many other places here.

And so we begin, only slowly, to know where we live. And to see, hear, smell people living in this way rattles the mind, it shatters the sensibilities. To be confronted by it, to be so close to it, and to be standing there in it with a £400 digital camera in one pocket, and a wallet packed with a thick stack of 4,000 rupees (an awful lot of money for these people!) in the other, makes me want to throw up.

I see a child, a seven-, eight-year old kid coming along the bumpy, muddy path on a rusted bike returning from the nearest (dirty) water hole, laden with spilling buckets filled with contaminated water because that's the only water they've got. And then to stand there as he passes by and to know, to really know, that the mere satisfaction of this child's thirst is fraught with danger, genuine life-threatening danger, is utterly heart-breaking.

As we walk along the pathways, these small, twisting alleyways, the broken doors are all open to let in any fresher air there may be, but they also let in me: these doors become holes that expose the material poverty of the lives lived within. Against my better judgement, and in fear, perhaps, of catching someone's eye, I feel my eyes fall to the left and I see inside and from the gloom come images of the empty, broken scraps of furniture, a child standing in a bucket of dirty water being washed; clothes, mere rags, hanging limply on faded, scratched chairs to dry after they too were washed in this same, dirty water. I see an old man, bent double over an old, lopsided table repairing old sandals, most likely his only footwear (but many have none). And a young woman, maybe twenty-five, stands in another doorway, framed by its faded green paint, a child of maybe two or three held in her arms, and the child is quiet. As we walk past she smiles, and we smile too, and for the first time I know that even though I am in the midst of such deep, distressing poverty, I am also deep within the measure of this peoples' humanity.

For all of these people have profound dignity, they have humour, they smile, they constantly smile. Children come up to us and want to shake our hand, so we do, and then their small, fragile bodies shake with glee and laughter, their voices toned with amazement and wonder (we're such a sight to them! No one ever comes this way!). And yet these same, fabulous people have to piss and shit in the streets, squat over a cesspit, in open view of the whole damned world – if the world could be damned enough to cast them a glance.

If someone has nothing, not a home, not water that won't kill them, not filth-infested clothes, not a toilet, not a place to belong to, what more can be taken from them? What more does a society want to deny them? They have no access to healthcare, welfare, education, information, employment, nutritious food, healthy water, none of it. There are no records of their lives, they appear on no census, no doctor's records, no official reports, nowhere; nowhere do they appear other than as shadows in the dirtiest streets.

And then, as quickly as we arrived here, we emerge back into the general shabbiness of the rest of Chennai, which seems so tolerable compared to what is now only "back there". And O is talking, but I am not listening, because I am trying to think, trying to find out what just happened, trying to find a way into it even though for the sake of my sanity I want to get the hell away from it.

This much I do know: I wanted to see it, hear it, smell it, I wanted its stink in my face because to me, to deny it is to be a liar. But then, to know it and then to turn and walk away is, I feel, a shameful cruelty and a denial of their very humanity. And again, to live so royally, so grandly in a land of such catastrophic deprivation makes my skin crawl. And I want none of it.

And then we strolled along the beach and then we strolled back and then I went to work and worked all night, and then the next day I went home, and I slept fitfully, and I dreamt. And in my dream, I went down to the riverbank here in Chennai, down to where the worst of it all suffers.

In my dream I walked past the cow-dung houses (these huts really are made of cow-dung!), past the stench of human and animal waste, and I went down to the water's edge.

And at the water's edge was a wild man (and he's real too! He wears dark blue clothes and has a thick jet black beard and he lives on the rubbish by the bridge over the river Cooum (one of the most polluted bodies of water on Earth). I sometimes see him looking out at the world going past, at me going past). He was sitting on an upturned bucket, staring out across the river. I knelt down next to him, the black thick water bubbling at my shoes. He did not look at me, and I did not look at him. I stared desperately into the dark flow before me.

And I said, "How long have you been living here?", and he said, "For over a thousand years." And I said, "Why don't you leave?" and he said, "Here only in the whole world am I allowed at least to live. So I remain, among people who here only in the whole world are allowed at most to die."

Then there was a silence, except for the squawk of crows and the odd cough or two from a child or two from within the cow-dung houses. He spoke again: "I have seen things that will never fade, I have heard things that will never fall silent, and I have felt things that will hurt me for all time." And then he did turn to me, and look at me, and I did turn to him and I saw into his bright, striking blue eyes. And then he said, "If you could lick my heart, it would poison you."

And then I woke up with a start, I jumped awake at that point, and I'm so glad I awoke at that point, because that last phrase frightened me, and it frightened me because that last phrase is real, it lives in the real world and it belongs to Yitzhak Zuckermann, a magnificent, noble human being, who was one of the chief instigators and fighters of the Warsaw ghetto revolt of Feb-April 1943 during the Second World War when the Jewish community that remained in the ghetto, after so many had before been murdered so brutally in the murder camp Treblinka, rose up against their oppressors, the murderers, and fought back with extraordinary dignity and determination to preserve, if not their lives, then their humanity. But Yitzhak survived that, and he survived so much more before, and afterwards he said what he said because of what he saw, and heard and felt, because of what he knew.

And I in my dream, and now in my writing, I do not mean to demean his words, to take his words in vain and use them in such a different context, in such a different way, because I do not mean to equate that, the Holocaust, with this, the slums; not that, the deliberate, industrial slaughter of millions of innocents with this, the slow, casual elimination of millions of poor people across the face of the earth. Or do I? Should I?

Here I am without a mouth; I am mute; I have no voice. Why? Because I'm standing here yelling and screaming in the midst of a massive moral vacuum.

EQUALITY FOR ALL LIFE: A REFLECTION

Look around you, and see the world. A bright, blue-green globe of life that shines by the reflected light of its parent star, our sun. Our world. But it is not... yet... the wonderful world that it can be.

As a species we have proven ourselves, through the centuries, of being capable of the most shocking cruelties and hatreds, against our kind and against that great number of other lives with whom we share this fragile planet. Our violence, our aggression, our blooding of the world has done great harm to ourselves and to so many, many others who have felt the blow of the dark hand of humanity.

But it does not have to be so.

We are capable of great passions, our emotions stir within us and rouse us to great thoughts and deeds; we can open our hearts, minds and souls to wisdom and compassion, we can, in wonder, regard the billions who are our fellow travellers on this world through space and time, and we can, if we want, let love be the light of our lives.

We can open our eyes in a new dawn onto the best of all possible worlds... if

and it's a big IF...

we dare to believe in love in its most perfect form and we dare to *be* love, expressed completely and absolutely, without compromise or hesitation, without condition, limitation or mitigation... love given to all deservedly and unreservedly...

love: the great equaliser, creating a world, finally, where equality for all life is the defining, the refining emotion of our life...

And in this world we will learn to know what equality for all lives really means. It means that we will know, as I know now, that I am the equal of every other life in this world... and they are all the equal of me...

It means that I know that as I am worthy of my life so too every one of these others is equally worthy of their lives...

We each have life and our lives are equal, each to each, equally, one another, deserving of our every breath and our share in the space and the time of our lives, our days and our nights beneath the sun and the moon, the great arc of the cosmic light

It means that I know that I am exactly the equal of the rat the runs along the forest floor, and he is absolutely, totally, the equal of me

And I am the same, the equal, of the chicken that picks and pecks at the ground below her feet, and she is truly, eye-to-eye, the same, the equal of me

It means that I am the same as the cod that darts this way and that through the dark, cold waters of the northern seas, and he is the same as me

He is worthy of his life, the beating of his heart, just as I am worthy of the beating of my heart... we are brothers beneath our skin, equal and the same in the beating of our hearts

It means that I am equal to, precisely equal to, the cow and the pig and the sheep, not better than them, and they are not worse than me, we are the same, the lamb and I, the piglet and I, the calf and I, all of us the same, of one substance born, the stuff of stars, and all warmed by the one light of our one sun... we are one...

I am the lion and the wolf and the horse, the bear, the eagle and the gorilla, and they are me… and so too is the mouse, the crab and the scorpion, the lizard, the toad and the squid, together with the octopus, the shark and the whale, and the seal, and the walrus, the lobster and the turkey…

It makes no difference to me, because they are no different to me

Whether they creep, swim or fly… we are all the same beneath the blue of the sky

All of us the children of our Mother Earth, all of us equal in her maternal eye

This is the meaning of perfect love: that we are all, all of us, every life on Earth, equally as worthy as one another, equally deserving of the life we have, the breath we take, the freedom we crave, the safety we covet, the comfort we wish for, the love we desire…

When we aspire to be the equal of every other… we reach the height of perfection, express the finest intention, and convey the wisest reflection of our role, our place, our space in the fabric of the world and the cosmos

The meaning of our life is given when the love that we have is offered, always and every time, to every life, and every moment of our life is taken as a chance to love

AFTER WORDS

When all is read and everything is said, I hope that things are done.

I write and speak so that actions can result from the words being read and heard, that hopefully at least some of these words can resonate with our innate sense of justice and common concern for others and motivate us towards wanting to create a better, kinder, more compassionate world.

Words, by themselves, are meaningless. They need and must move us and change us in some way and inspire us to act. It is true that actions can speak louder than a thousand words, and I have written something in the order of 75,000 words in this book – I can only hope and imagine what thousands and thousands of acts of compassion and kindness would mean for those who presently fear and hurt because of how badly we think and how badly we act towards them.

I write in the hope that the generosity, the thoughtfulness and the love of which we are all capable will win through and defeat our apathy, the lethargy that prevents us from being moved to granting help and giving freedom and life to the uncountable numbers of other Earthlings who live here with us, and who, like us, cannot live anywhere else and who, just like us, deserve protection from harm and the right to live their lives free from injustice, exploitation and violence.

We seem to be so many, us inhabitants of Earth, but compared to the great number of planets and stars and galaxies that extend further in space than time itself can let us see, we are few. Our fate is precarious, dependent as it is on the proper balance of gases in the atmosphere, the health of our seas and oceans, and a diversity of ecologies to create the right environment for our kind. Our survival is not a given and technology will not save us from every bad habit we have, every destructive act we commit, every despoiling of our home we impose in our folly.

There is no-one else, anywhere else, to whom we can turn and ask for help if we cause our home world so much damage, so much devastation, that neither we nor so many others can continue to live. Our death will be a lonely end and no-one will come to comfort us in our final years and bear witness to our last breath. No flowers will be offered in remembrance.

After all of the promise offered by our finest achievements and our grandest gestures, and our confidence in our ability to overcome all challenges, it will be a grave tragedy if we, in our desire for "success" (whatever that may mean) allow selfishness to outgrow our wisdom and choose to dominate rather than co-operate, and fail to heed the call of our hearts to compassion, and prefer to crush underfoot any who stand (apparently) in our way.

Our strength does not lie in our ability to destroy in pursuit of our self-interest but in our capacity to create opportunity and space for all to live and live peacefully, sharing the chance for all to grow healthily and comfortably from the riches offered by our home world.

No man or woman or child is an island, and humanity cannot exist in complete isolation from other species; life is sustained only by the chatter of billions of lives in deep and complex interaction, a planet-wide conversation where everyone must have a voice. If we destroy everyone else that surrounds us then we destroy ourselves too and the song of life will end and the Earth will fall silent once more as in its earliest days.

When we speak we must speak not only for ourselves but for others too; our call should be a chorus, the sound of a global community talking as one. As we speak our words should echo the needs of everyone. We speak for all or we speak for none.

Whether we have a future depends absolutely on the answer we personally choose to give to the question, "Who speaks for Earthlings?"

Printed in Great Britain
by Amazon.co.uk, Ltd.,
Marston Gate.